The Christian Marriage

A Sixfold Covenant
of Love-Motivated Servanthood

The Christian Marriage

A Sixfold Covenant
of Love-Motivated Servanthood

Chris S. Sherrerd

Treasure House

An Imprint of
Destiny Image
P.O. Box 310
Shippensburg, PA 17257

"For where your treasure is
there will your heart be also." Matthew 6:21

ISBN 1-56043-806-1

For Worldwide Distribution
Printed in the U.S.A.

Treasure House books are available through these fine distributors outside the United States:

Christian Growth, Inc. Jalan Kilang-Timor, Singapore 0315	Successful Christian Living Capetown, Rep. of South Africa
Lifestream Nottingham, England	Vision Resources Ponsonby, Auckland, New Zealand
Rhema Ministries Trading Randburg, South Africa	WA Buchanan Company Geebung, Queensland, Australia
Salvation Book Centre Petaling, Jaya, Malaysia	Word Alive Niverville, Manitoba, Canada

Inside the U.S., call toll free to order:
1-800-722-6774

Many writers change the exact transliterations of Hebrew words into more pronounceable forms. Nobody knows how ancient Hebrew was pronounced, since it ceased twice in history to be a spoken language. The more precise way to transliterate Hebrew is to use capital letters to represent actual Hebrew letters, with lowercase letters added in certain cases. The following chart gives the Hebrew transliterations used throughout this book.

Hebrew Letter	English Representation	Hebrew Letter	English Representation
א	Ah	ל	L
ב	B	מ (ם)	M
ג	G	נ (ן)	N
ד	D	ס	S
ה	H	ע	I
ו	W	פ (ף)	Ph
ז	Z	צ (ץ)	Ts
ח	Ch	ק	Q
ט	T	ר	R
י	Y	ש	Sh
כ (ך)	K	ת	Th

For further information, write to:

Shulemite Christian Crusade, Inc.
Chris S. Sherrerd
2 Deerwood Dr.
P.O. Box 4977,
Clinton, NJ 08809-0977

Dedication

This volume, and the other six volumes of the series *Where Do You Fit In? Practical Commitments in the Body of Christ,* is dedicated to the leaders of the new wave of God that is beginning to move throughout the Body of Christ. Throughout the Body, there is a general awareness that our Lord Christ Jesus is now about to do something drastically new among us. Many are desperately seeking to know how the Lord wants us to prepare for it.

It is the leaders who must (a) personally live this message first; (b) teach it to others so they may properly respond to the Lord in the days ahead; (c) discern the spiritual needs of fellow Christians and discover how they can benefit by this message; and (d) help others walk in this message as they respond to God's voice.

Acknowledgments

My first acknowledgment is to our Lord Christ Jesus, for: (a) imparting to me His spiritual reality and the many insights of His ways, as I studied His Word; (b) leading and empowering me explicitly as I personally walked through my inner heart healing, and hence became able to understand and share it; (c) making it possible for me to take the time to commit it all to writing, and anointing me as I did; and (d) being patient with me as I removed, hopefully, most of the ways Chris polluted Christ in the manuscripts.

My second acknowledgment is to my wife Dottie, a godly woman, who with great love, patience, and fortitude has worked with me over the years to actually walk in this.

My third acknowledgment is to my prayer partner during much of the writing, Alan Youngblood, for (a) supporting me in prayer during the darkest moments of my walk through a major portion of my inner heart healing, and (b) giving me constant encouragement and correction.

My fourth acknowledgment is to my pastor, Rev. Mark Boucher, for spending a considerable amount of time critiquing the first draft of the manuscript for this volume, and for giving me many very helpful comments and suggestions.

My fifth acknowledgment is to the staff at Destiny Image Publishers for making this book possible. My special thanks go to Larry Walker for his excellent work in abridging and rewriting my original manuscript to make it readable; to Tony Laidig for designing a cover that illustrated my idea; and to Eva Ball for patiently facilitating the entire publication process.

Chris S. Sherrerd

Contents

Preface

Late in the spring of 1992, I attended my fortieth college reunion. One thing impressed me above all else: Of the dozen or so men I was closest to during my undergraduate years, not a single one of us had been divorced! One had been widowed and another had never married, but the rest of us were accompanied by our original spouses.

The divorce rate for "the class of 1952" was low, but the class that graduated only 15 years later had a 50 percent divorce rate! Many from the graduating class of 1982 have not even married. These statistics apply almost equally to Christians and non-Christians! Almost anything goes today, with abortion touted as a legal "solution" to unwed pregnancies.

I grew up in a "sandwich" generation during the Great Depression and the early years of World War II. Our prime adult years coincided with the two decades of greatest economic, social, and intellectual freedom ever known in human history: the 1950's and 1960's in America.

Marriage was an economic necessity for the generations before us. Most women had no means of support outside of marriage, and the workload to support a family was more than the husband alone could handle. Yet, for the generations after us, marriage became but a "temporary" phase of life (if, that is, one discounts the terrible sufferings resulting from the dysfunctional traumas of divorce).

My generation seems to have been one of the last with more-or-less stable marriages. Why has that been lost with the two generations born since then, namely the "baby boomers" and their children?

Marriages generally deteriorate when at least two of the following destructive attitudes pertain:

1. *Self-seeking by each spouse.* Trouble arises when one spouse expects the other spouse to meet emotional and spiritual needs in ways he or she is not able to.

2. *Self-protecting by each spouse.* Damage occurs when spouses deploy "distancing strategies" to avoid what appear to be "life-threatening" hurts from the other spouse. (These are usually dysfunctionally-rooted.)

3. *Each spouse holds a distorted—if not an outright erroneous—understanding of human sexuality.* This happens when a husband does not know how, or simply refuses, to give his wife the unconditional acceptance, love, and security she really needs. It also happens when a wife does not know how, or simply refuses, to respect and accept her

husband, as a man, and what he seeks to do with and for her.

What has happened in America since the early 1950's that has caused such widespread destruction in marriage relationships?

I suggest the reasons may be found in three social forces in America that were rooted in the 1940's and 1950's. They began to significantly impact our culture in the 1960's, after my generation's moral values had already taken root in our lives.

The Playboy mentality. Playboy Magazine first appeared in December 1953, and it initially targeted young college men who, one generation later, became the leaders of our society and government.

The magazine itself wasn't the point of significance—the thing that transformed our society was the mentality it represented, the whole philosophy of life, a paradigm. Male-female relationships, rather than being viewed and honored as the core of our society, now were viewed as existing solely for *hedonistic self-seeking.* The new way of thinking was, "If one partner does not satisfy, try another." Today, that paradigm permeates our entire culture, and has intensely reinforced other destructive attitudes.

Social rootlessness. The suburban syndrome (of "the split-level trap") has also transformed our society. Our jobs have required us to move to new geographic locations every few years. During the first four years of our marriage, for example, my wife and I lived in six different locations.

For the most part, American families have lost the strong family ties which my generation once knew and lived by. Women no longer support other women throughout the trials of life—their friendships don't last long enough, and their schedules don't permit it. We no longer develop close, lifelong friendships, for each time we meet a friend and grow close, we have to move again.

Workaholic fathers, who are often absent on business trips while trying to survive in a more aggressive and hostile business world, have become the norm. This puts intense emotional strains on marriage relationships, and intensely reinforces other destructive attitudes.

But these two factors, working against stable marriage relationships as they do, cannot account alone for the near-total breakdown of morals in America. My generation was also affected by these social factors. Yes, we suffered from them too, and we also had our share of dysfunctionally-rooted self-seeking and self-protecting strategies. Yet the avalanche of broken marriages did not catch us. A third social factor entered the picture to act as a catalyst, and to amplify the destructive forces clawing away at America's marriages.

Rejection of God and the Bible. This third destructive social factor grew out of our abuse of our new economic, social, and intellectual freedom. We turned our backs on God. People decided they would no longer be "tied down" to the beliefs, value systems, and biblical principles of the preceding generation (or so they thought). Intellectual atheism, as part of our new national religion of scientific humanism, replaced biblical patterns and principles in the thinking of virtually the entire nation. Christians as well as non-Christians embraced the "open-minded" self-orientated views of the godless.

As a result of this three-pronged assault, the Christian concept of total commitment to servanthood in marriage, embraced by my generation, was annihilated. Or was it? We can now see that this "old, outdated concept," so foreign to our thinking, is not only still very valid (it actually works!), but it is also the most beautiful of all conceivable human relationships available to us!

However, *it still requires* that our individual life styles and our Christian marriages become fully Christ-centered. Alas, that is not the case today for the vast majority of Christians in the "Western" nations—even "Spirit-filled Christians." We have accumulated many years of teachings and literature on the Christian marriage in the Body of Christ worldwide, yet few of us have begun to lay hold of the Bible's wealth of admonitions.

We have allowed the Playboy mentality to rob us of our personhood as women and our masculinity as men rather than regard our marriage relationship as the point where Christ empowers each to be a love-motivated servant of the other! We have substituted a legalistic concept of unemotional authority in place of God's view that "headship" and "submission" are actually *forms of servanthood* in the context of covering and rapport (those forms of servanthood being unique to masculinity and femininity).

We view our marriage partners as people who will meet our needs—although our inner needs can only be met by the indwelling Holy Spirit of Christ Jesus—rather than truly *respecting* one another. Though most of us successfully give an outward appearance of having a real

"Christian" marriage, most of us live at an emotional distance from one another, or exist in a joyless state of emotional divorce. Those of us who do recognize that our marriages are not all our Lord has for us, and sincerely repent, still don't know how to improve them.

Many motivations are behind this "distancing," but the two most prevalent in our culture are the following:

1. Wives, and women in general, fostering disrespect, distrust, and even bitterness against men.

2. Husbands, and men in general, fostering an abysmally low self-image, low self-esteem, and a sense of inadequacy as men.

These two problems are particularly widespread today because of "the Playboy mentality" that has permeated our culture now for almost 40 years. This was complicated by the associated mentality of its backlash, the "feminist movement." This mentality literally dehumanizes women and emasculates men.

These things are further intensified by painful experiences in our past, often during childhood, if not later. Unless we get rid of these two attitudes, they will drive and affect our interpersonal behavior for the rest of our lives. They are forms of sin, and we must repent of them by faith according to biblical principles.

These syndromes take on very different forms and levels of intensity from individual to individual, depending upon particular personality traits and marriage circumstances. They are accompanied by what I call *embedded emotional empowerments*. They are *embedded* because they are usually below the surface of our cognitive awareness. They are *emotional*, not rational. They are *empowerments* because they do not only exist; they *drive us*. They constantly work to destroy the marriage relationship through "distancing."

For example, when a wife tries to reach out to her husband in genuine love, seeking intimacy (or even trying to reach out to him for ordinary communication), he may prevent her from coming too close by erecting a barrier of some sort. He does this so she will not get close enough emotionally or rationally to discover that he feels inadequate as a husband and father (even though she may already sense that). That barrier hurts her deeply.

Likewise, when the husband tries to reach out to his wife in genuine love, seeking appreciation (or even trying to reach out to her for ordinary communication), she may prevent him from coming too close by erecting a barrier of some sort. She does this so he will not get close enough emotionally or intellectually to hurt, abuse, or humiliate her. That barrier hurts him deeply as well.

Because these drives are *embedded* emotions, both partners are usually unaware of their actions. Even more importantly, they are totally unaware that they are deeply hurting the other spouse.

Christians do a fairly good job of coping on the surface, for the most part. We try to apprehend Christ and His promises by faith; we ask Him to reveal hidden sin in our lives. We attend seminars, conferences, and Bible studies that address the marriage relationship, and we try to apply those lessons to ourselves. As a result, we acquire some degree of communication and rapport, which gives us some abatement of the pain.

Unfortunately, we also substitute other activities to alleviate our frustrations as we seek acceptance, appreciation, intimacy, and harmony. These things only serve to temporarily mask hurts that are still there. As the years pass, and children come along, the hurts accumulate and fester. Though friends and acquaintances don't know it, those hurts become unbearable. Each partner is deeply hurting the other, typically without realizing it. Many of us feel that our spouse has so often, so persistently, so impersonally failed to meet our needs, or even to fulfill basic responsibilities, that we see no hope. Our Christian faith may be beginning to waver. We ask why the Lord, whom we indeed love and have been trying to obey all these years, has allowed our lives to disintegrate. What is wrong? This is the process of the *dysfunctional downward spiral* of the marriage relationship.

Like alcoholics in denial, marriage partners (including Christian couples) rarely seek help until they hit rock bottom and have no other hope. Eventually, the Lord may allow a crisis to occur in order to force their hand (though they probably will not recognize the Lord in it). Whether through a loss of job or health, intolerable physical abuse, a wayward (or suicidal) child, or whatever, these couples may finally be driven to seek help.

Where do these couples go for help? Since the root cause of the problem is sin in each partner in the form of embedded emotionally empowered distancing strategies, most psychological counseling can't get to those *root* causes and really help. That form of counseling may address surface symptoms, and provide yet another temporary respite. Even group therapeutic approaches provide that by helping us understand ourselves a little better, and by providing a sense of acceptance by fellow Christians (though that is difficult for men). But since those therapies only touch the surface symptoms, allowing the root issues to run rampant, it is inevitable that we will encounter yet another crisis down the road.

It is far better and more biblical to submit to Christian counseling, where the indwelling Holy Spirit of Christ Jesus truly guides the counselor.

But even then, when a couple in trouble turns to counseling for help, they do so primarily with the hope and expectation that the counselor will help the *other* spouse change his or her hurting ways. That's understandable. However, if the Lord is truly directing the healing of the marriage, that is not His way! He insists that each of us depend on Him to change *ourselves*, whether He changes the other person or not (although He's after that also)! That's because He is determined to do far more than heal a marriage; He wants to root out the sin in our lives that is hurting the marriage relationship in the first place!

He does this by confronting us in ways that force us to align our human wills (husband and wife) with His. God uses tribulations and challenges in our lives to actually strengthen our faith. This is especially true for Christian couples who will be used by the Lord in some form of ministry of Christian service!

God carefully removes every alternative but two: (a) We can choose to go all the way in Christ, or (b) continue to allow the marriage relationship to be destroyed, with every life involved to suffer beyond our expectations. There is no third alternative.

The choice to "go all the way in Christ" actually has four individual responsibilities inherent within it:

1. I must unreservedly determine, from here on, to always respond to my spouse as Christ would have me respond. I am not to respond out of self-seeking and/or self-protecting motives.

2. I must so act in expectation, knowing God will empower me to respond His way in all cases.

3. I must utterly abandon myself to God, and depend upon Him to ensure that the results of my new way will be in my best interests.

4. I must totally release my spouse to Him, knowing that He alone must deal with him or her (with no "help" from me), as He alone chooses!

That four-pronged choice must be made separately by each spouse, and separately from those of our spouse. This is a hard choice for most of us, but it is one choice we must make. If we don't, then by default, we have made the choice of "self," which will continue to lead to our destruction! No Christian friend, pastor, or counselor, nor our spouse, can crawl into our heads and make the choice for us! For many of us, the crisis in our marriages and personal lives is too pressing for us to wait any longer.

What is going to be your choice? If you want to gain a detailed understanding of all our Lord desires for your marriage, and how you can achieve it, then this book is for you.

The bottom line is that each marriage partner must be the love-motivated servant of the other, as the indwelling Holy Spirit of Christ Jesus empowers them. That is the missing gap in the Body of Christ today. Christians of the generations before us would see nothing new in this. An old cross-stitched sampler reads "HOME SWEET HOME—Where Each Lives For The Other, And Both Live For God." So I do not have an innovative interpretation of Scripture: I'm restoring a godly truth that has been lost for many generations.

This book is the first of a series of seven volumes under the title, *Where Do You Fit In?* It describes the current move of God as an outpouring of the Holy Spirit of Christ Jesus on God's people, *not* for revival *per se*, but for the *purging* of His Body so a significant number of us can be used as His instruments for subsequent revivals. With that vision in mind, the series examines what our Lord is doing in His Body, and what we need to do and become to best yield to His purposes.

Leonard Ravenhill wrote, "The disparity between the New Testament church in the book of Acts and what passes for the church today is appalling."[1] The form and nature of current Christianity is patterned according to the sin of Christian denominationalism, a paradigm or way of thinking whose captivity of Christianity dates back to the second through fourth centuries of the Christian Era. Denominationalism and the Body of Christ are totally antithetical. Denominationalism, based on doctrine, theology, and social/political institutionalism, focuses on "natural" functioning in this physical world, whereas the Body of Christ focuses on our functioning in the spiritual world by the power of the indwelling Holy Spirit of Christ Jesus.

This Volume I addresses our marriage relationships, the most crucial area for the purging work of the Holy Spirit within the Body of Christ today. Volume II delineates several dozen biblical portraits of three general levels of the maturing process in our individual relationships with Christ. Volume III delineates 12 parallel stages of the corporate maturation of the Body of Christ (right now, we are functioning at "stage four" at best). In Volumes IV and V we study many foundational aspects of our relationship to Him *as a spiritual reality*, and with one another in local social contexts. Volume VI examines our eschatological vision for these purging moves of the Holy Spirit. Volume VII exposes the many current forms of deception common within the Body of Christ today.

End Notes

1. Ravenhill, Leonard. *Revival God's Way* (Minneapolis, MN: Bethany House Publishers, 3rd Printing, 1986), p. 10. Copyright © 1986 by Bethany House Publishers.

Foreword

Time being the precious commodity that it is, when I pick up a book on marriage, I don't want to just go over "reruns." I ask myself two questions about a book: "How can I learn from this to help others?" and, "How can my own life and marriage be helped by this?"

In *The Christian Marriage*, Chris Sherrerd has done a wonderful service for the Body of Christ. God has used him to produce a tool that will better equip us to minister to others as well as enhance our own marriages. Chris intends for both husband and wife to grasp the significance of "Christ in us," and to live out their marriage in the Holy of Holies presence of God.

The theme of this book needs to be shouted from the housetops of America: *Marriage is a covenant of love-motivated servanthood, where each can be freed and empowered by the Holy Spirit to minister to the other!*

I am privileged to know Chris as a friend and partner in prayer. Jesus Christ is his Lord, and the desire of his heart is to know Christ more intimately. The fruit of his life is evident in the loving, stable relationship he has with his wife Dottie, and in the beautiful Christlike attitudes of his two daughters, Christie and Mary Beth.

In my ministry, the hardest and most heartbreaking experiences have been seeing some Christian marriages become emotionally or legally divorced. As hard as we might try in the Lord, we can't salvage all marriages. *The Christian Marriage* is a resource that has greatly enhanced my ability to understand God's love and grace for marriages, and it has helped me understand why some marriages fail. I have truly been helped by this book—as a person and as a pastor. Thank you, Chris, for your labor of love!

Pastor Mark Boucher

Part I

Created Male and Female
Unto Servanthood

In order to understand what a fully Christ-centered marriage relationship should be and what is required of us to achieve it, we need to start with a study of human nature (including human sexuality) as we were originally created. We also need to look at how our created natures have been so distorted by the Fall, and specifically what salvation/sanctification steps are necessary for our recovery. How can we understand the dynamics of our interpersonal relationships without an understanding of what and who we intrinsically are?

Chapter One

Created for Servanthood

All true doctrines of salvation in Christ are based upon divine creation: They make no sense outside of creation. This applies particularly to the nature of man and man's relationship with God from creation onward.

> *Then God* [i.e., the Godhead] *said, "Let Us make man in **Our image**, according to Our likeness... ."* *And God created man in **His own image**.... For in the image of God He made man* (Genesis 1:26-27; 9:6b).

1. Yes, Created!

If we are to genuinely experience and understand what it is to "walk in the Spirit," then we must understand the nature of man and the world as created by God. Why did God create mankind in the first place? Our being created "in Our image" means, among other things, that we were created "in the image" of the Godhead's mer tality, interests, personal objectives, desires, goals, a emphases of operation. The plan of the Godhead is each member to freely choose to live and function for the other members of His family.

God wants spiritual offspring in whom He can entrust responsibility over the other portions of His creation. That is why He has (a) created us with a free choice; (b) confronted us with a real, practicable choice and challenge; (c) allowed us to try that alternative; (d) showed us that His way of totally self-abandoning love is much more desirable to us than self-seeking; and (e) demonstrated His love for the human race by giving up His Son's life to redeem us from our depraved state and restore us into oneness with Him.

This description is oversimplified and understated, but it captures the essence of the single plan behind God's dealings with mankind during the first 6,000 years of human history. This carefully focused plan overrode all dispensations; He did not develop a "separate plan" for each dispensation. Over time, God has presented *successive revelations* of His plan for us through successive covenant relationships with men and women, but His plan has never changed. He always calls His children afresh to seek Him that He may deepen His revelations of Himself (in Christ Jesus) and His ways to mankind. God is never static.

In His Image

The Hebrew word for "image" or "likeness" in these passages is *TsLM*, which means "of the same form, particularly in appearance." It refers to more than mere outward appearance; it describes the very nature of the subject of the "image." In Genesis 3:22, God confirmed the depth of our similarity to His nature when He said, "Behold, the man has become like one of Us [the Godhead]."

Since man was created "in the image/likeness of God," n our race was originally created to have at least some he characteristics of God Himself. Since John 4:24

tells us that "God is spirit," then we know that man was originally created with at least some "spiritual" characteristics! God created man with a human spirit as well as with a soul, so he would have the ability to interact with the "spiritual" domain. Adam was actually created to live in both the "spiritual" domain with God, and to live in (and rule over) the "physical" domain of created creatures and things (Gen. 1:26-30; 2:15; 3:23).

The "spiritual world" of God is a very real domain that is of a higher order and is distinct from our physical domain. Two characteristics of God's "spiritual domain" are *incredible intelligence* and *power,* both of which may be manifested or demonstrated in our physical world.

Breath of Lives

Genesis 2:7 says, "Then the Lord God formed man of dust from the ground, and breathed into his [man's] nostrils the breath of life; and man became a living being." The Hebrew word for "life" (*ChYYM*) is in the *plural.* We received *more than one form of life* upon creation.

Life is the ability to dynamically *affect* our environment and to *respond* to it. Growth, adjustment, reproduction, and the many ways we have of controlling our environment, are all examples of such dynamic interactions.

2. Two Trees in the Garden

After studying William Law's writings *à la* Andrew Murray,[1,2] I realized that the *lives* that God gave man in Genesis 2:7 do not refer to man's domains or enviror ments, but rather to *God's purposes* for those forms of li Both *forms* of life involve dynamic interactions with 7 the "spiritual" and "physical" domains or environm Yet they have *vastly different purposes and effects*' two purposes are clearly depicted in the "trees" of Genesis 2:8-9.[3]

> *And the Lord God planted a garden toward the east, in Eden; and there He placed the man whom He had formed. And out of the ground the Lord God caused to grow every tree that is pleasing to the sight and good for food; the tree of life also in the midst of the garden, and the tree of the knowledge of good and evil* (Genesis 2:8-9).

The difference between spiritual and soulish living is the same as the difference between living according to the "tree of life" and the "tree of the knowledge of good and evil." Christ's indwelling is our "tree of life"; self-seeking is our "tree of knowledge." That is, the life of Christ indwelling is represented by the "tree of life" in Genesis 2:9, demonstrated in God's life of goodness, righteousness, and love which ever seeks to serve others. The "tree of the knowledge of good and evil," which Adam and Eve were forbidden to taste, represents man's innate potential for a life of self-seeking—apart from God's provision. Both forms of life involve both domains or environments we dwell in: the "spiritual" and the "physical."

Again the first "form of life" means living by Christ's indwelling. The real meaning of "eternal life" for us as Christians is that Christ is "doing the living" in and through us. This can only happen as we yield to Him. When He *does the doing*, we only act to meet the needs of others (particularly those of our spouse). We do not seek to have our needs met by our own efforts because He does that for us through others.

The second "form of life" simply means living by self. fact is that you and I are still being confronted by the same "great temptation" that Adam and Eve faced in the beginning! The root issue, according to Andrew Murray in his book, *The Spirit of Christ*, is an *unyielding self*.[4]

God created each of us with the potential to *choose* between the "trees" of the Christ-life and the self-seeking life. Prior to their fall, Adam and Eve chose to partake of the "tree of life" instead of the self-seeking life. This is a picture of God's perfect intent for us today.

To the extent that we do *not* live according to the "tree of life" of Christ's indwelling, then *by default* we have chosen to live by the "tree of knowledge" through our own self-seeking efforts. (This applies to both the unregenerate and the "nominal" or "legalistic" evangelical Christian!) The issue is *Christ's continual indwelling*, not just His act of paying the penalty for our sins and sealing our eternal destiny through His "one-time" death on Calvary.

Christianity has been taken captive by a pervasive spirit of denominationalism.[5] This is a form of religion which encourages bondage to law and guilt, the very things Jesus freed us from when He died on the cross! The fruit of this bondage is *spiritual impotence* and *frustration*, which leads to discouragement, loss of vision, and a lukewarm love.

The concept of the "Law," or living by rules and outward guidelines of righteousness, is associated with the "tree of the knowledge of good and evil." Most Christians believe in the New Testament (Covenant) doctrine of eternal life through Christ's indwelling, yet they actually walk in the spirit of law. Rick Joyner, in his book, *There Were Two Trees In The Garden*, points out this:

> ...through the Law we derive our knowledge of good and evil. We may wonder how this knowledg brings death until we see the fruit. The knowled

of good and evil kills us by distracting us from the One who is the source of life: the Tree of Life—Jesus. The Tree of Knowledge causes us to focus our attention upon ourselves. Sin is empowered by the law; not just because the evil is revealed but the good as well.[6]

3. Human Spiritual Needs

God's created world is maintained with needs and functions by needs. Every created entity, even if it seems to be complete in itself, *needs* something from other entities to fulfill its role or purpose in God's creation. For example, male and female need one another for companionship and reproduction. People need each other for economic and social benefits. Man needs God for inner fulfillment and peace, and for the power to fulfill his God-given purpose. This interrelationship of needs continues *ad infinitum*.

Our Creator God has made Himself available to all who seek Him, first through the Edenic "tree of life" (Gen. 2:9; 3:8), and now through Christ. This order of divine need-fulfillment reflects the glory of the life of God. He imparted His life of goodness, righteousness, and love to our first ancestor at creation, and now it is continuously available to us through the Tree (source) of Life, Jesus Christ.

This brings us to a further, significant way in which we are created "in the image of the Godhead"—we have been created to *serve* others, just as all members of the Godhead live to serve the others. And to serve out of the motive of love, not duty. Furthermore, this need for us to function in love—motivated servanthood is ingrained in our human *spirit*. This love-motivated servanthood among men and women is nothing less than the essence eternal life from God.

Since we are created for love-motivated servanthood, our human spirits have specific needs that must be filled for us to function as such. More specifically, our human spirits have three areas of needs related to servanthood:

1. We need to be valued as a servant.

2. We need to have a sense of significance, purpose, and way of serving.

3. We need to have others receive our servanthood.

When we are in Christ, He meets these needs, and we are truly in peace. But when we are under the Adamic curse, we try (inevitably in vain) to fulfill these needs through our own self-seeking efforts to manipulate others. This produces disappointments and leads to intense, and possibly life-threatening hurts.

These needs are among the most powerful long-term motivating forces in our lives. Unmet and uncontrolled, these needs can seriously hinder us from being all our Lord Christ Jesus wills for us. The basis of inner heart healing is the transference of our efforts to find fulfillment from *self-effort to Christ* as our Tree of Life.

4. The Human Spirit, Soul, and "Flesh"

Let us dwell further on this biblical concept of our (human) *spirit* as distinct from our *soul*. We develop this study in more depth in Volume II, *Profiles in Sanctification,* but we need to outline it here to better understand our human spiritual needs and their impact on human sexuality and interpersonal relationship. As Edwards[7] points out, even since early in the second century A.D., we have been taught the lies that man is only body and so without spirit, and that "spiritual" understanding mee only intellectual (doctrinal) understanding of the Sc tures. But the tripartite nature of the human psycholr makeup is one of the most essential and basic biblical understandings in the Christian life. God's discipline and chastening in our lives can only be explained in the context of three major and distinct aspects of the salvation of our three-part being.

Throughout the Old Testament, three distinct Hebrew words are used for spirit, soul, and flesh: *RWCh* (spirit), *NPhSh* (soul), and *BShR* (flesh). The corresponding Greek words in the New Testament are *pneuma* (spirit), *psuche* (soul), and *soma* (body). Paul often uses another Greek word, *sarx*, to refer to the "flesh"; (this refers to the *psychological power* of the appetites of the physical body. The New Testament Greek word used for the *entire* psychological makeup is *nuos* or *noos* (as in Ephesians 4:23), which literally means "our innermost sanctuary."

The Functions of the Human Spirit

The human spirit is the "seat" or center of man's God-consciousness. We alone, in the entire "animal kingdom," are created with the ability to be in two-way communication with God. The functions of the human spirit include the following:

1. *Intuition*—An ability to know the things of God, such as spiritual truths and other facts that can only be perceived in ways other than through the learning processes of the mind.

2. *Conscience*—An ability to know moral truths and to know God's will for us in speciic situations.

3. *Guilt*—God's way of warning us of our violations of His laws.

4. *Grievings*—Deep discomfort that causes us to seek God more earnestly.

5. *Yearnings*—Subtle motivation to abandon ourselves unto Him.

6. *Praise*—The drive to thank God for what He has done for and to us.

7. *Worship*—Actual spiritual union with God.

Since all of these functions are empowered and amplified by the Holy Spirit of Christ Jesus dwelling in our human spirits, the phrase "house of the Lord" *refers to our human spirit.* The full meaning of "grace" is the dwelling of His Holy Spirit in our human spirits.

The *human spirit* (denied by modern psychology) links man with the higher intelligences of Heaven. It is the highest part of man, and it is the seat of reception of, or "quickening" by, the Holy Spirit of Christ Jesus (1 Cor. 15:47). Problems arise because the soul and the flesh are normally more immediate (i.e., intense but short-term) forces in the human experience than the human spirit. These are in constant conflict with the Holy Spirit as He works through the human spirit.

The Functions of the Human Soul

The human soul is the seat of our self-consciousness, or that which *appears* to us to be "self" (the true and full "me" consists of the human spirit plus the soul, although the totality of *direct awareness* of self is in the soul alone). The functions of the soul include these four:

1. *The Mind*—The ability to consciously and rationally think.

2. *The Reason*—The ability to plan and calculate.

3. *The Emotions*—The ability to feel and emote

4. *The will* or Volition—The ability to deliberately determine and choose to act or not act.

The soul and the flesh are distinct. The soul, with its will function, actually controls. However, when the soul yields to the power of sin in the flesh, the results are the manifestations of the flesh. The flesh has to be "reckoned as dead" (i.e., having no influence over the soul) to be delivered from the power of sin (Rom. 6:11). This means that the "self-life of the soul" has to be dealt with by the cross—apart from and after basic regeneration (the initial "salvation" experience).

In our "natural" state (i.e., before complete sanctification by the Holy Spirit of Christ Jesus), our souls are in actual control of all we think and do. "Self" is the real king which is wrongfully enthroned in our "hearts." Satan, through sin-power, conducts warfare against the Holy Spirit to control our spirits. Christ is at work through His Holy Spirit in our human spirits to destroy the devil's works in us. The apostle Paul describes this warfare with phrases such as the "old man," the "old nature," and the "old creature." They refer to sin-power working through our flesh to dominate our souls; or the yielding of the soul to the power of sin (see Rom. 6:6; 1 Cor. 5:7-8; Eph. 4:22; Col. 3:9; 2 Pet. 1:9).

In contrast, the Bible also uses powerful phrases like "new man"; "new nature"; "new heart"; and "new creation" to describe the effects of the rule of the Holy Spirit through our human spirits, the result of yielding the soul to the spirit (see 2 Cor. 5:17; Gal. 6:15; Eph. 4:22-24; Col. 3:9-10).

The Flesh

The "flesh" (*sarx*) is the seat of man's world-consciousness. Though it contains all of our abilities to know the physical context of our lives, it describes much more than the human nervous and endocrine (hormonal) systems and the five physical senses. The "flesh" also includes the *influences of the physical senses* on the functions of the human soul.

The "flesh" or carnality is a real, distinct part of man. It is distinct from both the corporeal body and the soul, although it is closely linked to both. (That is why the Bible uses *sarx*, or "flesh," in addition to *soma*, the word for "body"). Carnality describes our bodily feelings, and it is closely linked with our nervous system.

Each of these three aspects of our psychological nature—the spirit, the soul, and the flesh—has a power of its own, apart from God, if it is not in Him. The flesh is the area of our lives of our most immediate awareness (see Eph. 2; Rom. 6). The soul has tremendous power in its own right, far more than we realize. The spirit possesses the power to communicate directly with the "spirit world"; with satanic spirits as well as with God.

Understanding "Spirit" and "Spiritual"

The realities of "spirit" and "spiritual" are totally beyond the conceptual capabilities of the natural "mind" and "natural" ways of thinking. Indeed, the vast majority of things most Christians believe to be "spiritual" are actually "soulish" or psychological.

The apostle Paul establishes a clear contrast between the things of God and the things of man in his letter to the Corinthians:

> Yet we do speak wisdom...the hidden wisdom, which God predestined before the ages...which none of the rulers of this age has understood...just as it is written, "Things which eye has not seen and ear h/

not heard, and which have not entered the heart of man...." For to us God revealed them through the Spirit...the thoughts of God no one knows except the Spirit of God. ...we also speak, not in words taught by human wisdom, but in those taught by the Spirit, combining spiritual thoughts with spiritual words. But a natural man does not accept the things of the Spirit of God; for they are foolishness to him, and he cannot understand them, because they are spiritually appraised. But he who is spiritual appraises all things... (1 Corinthians 2:6-11, 13-15).

We can only understand the Bible's teachings of "spiritual" things by thinking in vastly different ways than we do now. The "Law of Righteousness" is spiritual, and the only way to understand "the things of the Spirit" is through the Holy Spirit (see Rom. 8:4-7,9-11,16). Even with the help of the indwelling Holy Spirit of Christ Jesus, spiritual understanding comes gradually. We have to "grow" in them.

Every human thought, whether good or bad, radiates into the "spiritual domain." Our human spirits have the potential to explore, move about within, and influence that domain. However, if we fail to surrender all of our spiritual activities to the lordship of Christ Jesus, then we are headed for trouble. When men and women try to "be like God" on their own, they not only sin (in the same way Adam and Eve sinned), but they inevitably open themselves up to domination and control by the demonic forces of satan. Many young people today have discovered the deadly bondage and destruction awaiting those who wander into the dark spirit world of the occult, Eastern mysticism, New Age movement, and other forms of satanism.

5. Love vs. the Kingdom of Self

One thing that our souls cannot counterfeit or generate is genuine Christian love. *Agape* love is the one true proof of the working of the Holy Spirit of Christ Jesus in yielded lives. This attribute or characteristic lies totally outside of the capabilities of our souls.

Most of the "love" we experience is of the soul. "Love" comes in several forms, including *eros*, or passion love, which is fleshly and soulish in manifestation (though it originates in the human spirit); *storge*, or familial or "homey" love, which is soulish; *philea*, which is the love of truth, love of knowledge, love of high ideals, love for a "cause", or even love for the cause of "saving souls" (as distinct from *agape* love for the souls, *per se!*).

Eros love, or sexual passion itself, though a powerful force driving both the soul and flesh, actually originates in one's human spirit. Gordon Dalby points this out in his book *Father and Son* as well.[8] For example, suppose John experiences what the world calls "falling in love" [*eros* love] with Jane. Where does John's love for Jane come from? It's not from Jane; she does not "generate" and "transmit" it to John. In fact, she is even oblivious to it unless or until John somehow communicates his feelings to Jane (either through body language or words). Nor did it originate in John's soul (mind, emotions, and will); although it powerfully drives these soul functions. It did not originate in John's mind—love is intrinsically irrational. Nor did it originate in John's emotions either; h emotions *resulted* from his love, not caused his lo Finally John did not choose to "fall in love" with Jan "just happened." So where did *eros* love originate John's human *spirit*. It is totally subject to wha spiritual influences John is under at the time.[9]

Philea love is basically "the love of possessing something in common with another person." Virtually all of the "love" prevalent in "Spirit-filled" church circles today is *philea* love: We have Christ in common! *Philea* is a beautiful form of love created by God, but it has limitations. Because it is based on human soulish pleasure, soulish harmony, and fulfillment, it quickly vanishes when another perosn (particularly a fellow Christian) offends us.

Agape love motivates us to do everything in our ability to build up others. We build up their right relationship with God through Christ Jesus, their self-worth, self-respect, dignity, and personal fulfillment. In other words, *agape* love creates a desire to build up those around us to be everything God wills for them individually.

This *agape* love is for people. It is intensely personal, and it creates intense personal involvement with others. It leads us into a very costly form of servanthood because the people *most in need of **agape** love*, or the very ones who deserve it the least, are most likely the ones to *intensely reject* it (and us). *Agape* love is hard work. It requires our spending much time not only in intercessory prayer before God for others, but also in direct, interpersonal contact with them. It is dynamic, aggressive, responsible, and very specific in its applications.

One of the chief attributes of *agape* love is that it is totally unselfish. We "*agape*-love" another solely for that person's betterment, regardless of what we get out of it (which is often rejection). Undiluted *agape* love has the attitude that our neighbors are worth all we can do for them. They are even more worthy than we ourselves, and we will see them whole if it costs us our lives. Jesus hrist demonstrated this level of true *agape* love for us the cross.

Agape love is a *spiritual phenomenon* that is distinguished by properties exactly opposite to all that is soulish. Spiritual love is love for the other's sake, period! Soulish love seeks to gain something in return—to be loved, honored, or praised; to enhance the ego, and possibly the flesh.

Agape love is given solely for the benefit of the recipient, regardless of what happens to the giver. Because of the very nature of *agape* love, those who give it to others almost always experience sufferings, rejection, and great personal cost—even to the point of death. This is the result of Christ in the giver flowing out in the form of pure *agape* love to others.

Most Christians walk "in the Spirit" without *agape* love! Andrew Murray noted in *The Spirit of Christ* that the believers in the Corinthian church were enriched in all "spirituals," but without love:

> ...The natural powers of the soul—knowledge, faith, utterance—may be greatly affected, without self being yet fully surrendered; and how thus many of the gifts of the Spirit may be seen, while the chief of all, love, is sadly lacking....

> Let us learn the lesson and pray very fervently that God will teach it to His people, that a church or a Christian professing to having the Holy Spirit must prove it, in the first place, by the exhibition of a Christ-like Love.[10]

End Notes: Chapter One

1. Murray, Andrew. *Wholly for God* (Minneapolis, MN: Dimension Books, Bethany Fellowship, Inc., 1977), originally published in 1894.

2. Murray, Andrew. *Freedom From A Self-Centered Life: Dying To Self* (Minneapolis, MN: Dimension Books, Bethany Fellowship, Inc., 1977), originally published in 1898.

3. The Hebrew word for "tree" in this context is *EyTs*, from the verb root *EyTsHa*, which means "to be hard, firm, strong." In the garden of Eden, the idea is of an *EyTs* whose fruit is to be, or not to be, eaten; and that of a strong source or provider readily available to all who would partake of it.

4. Murray, Andrew. *The Spirit of Christ* (Minneapolis, MN: Bethany Fellowship, Inc., 1979), pp. 230-231. Copyright © 1979 by Bethany Fellowship, Inc.

5. Denominationalism is a paradigm or mentality of Christian religions wherein: (a) the person of Christ indwelling is replaced by philosophy and theology based on doctrines about Him; (b) the social structure of the Body of Christ is replaced by a religious organization; and (c) the social dynamics of Body members ministering to one another is replaced by a priesthood-vs.-laity order in which one or a few elite "priests" or "ministers" do all the

ministry, and the people simply provide the context and logistics for him or her. This error began to encrust Christianity before the end of the first century A.D., and by the mid-300's, it fully characterized the "visible" Christian Church. The Protestant Reformation over the past 450 years has not yet completely weaned us from it.

6. Joyner, Rick. *There Were Two Trees In The Garden* (Pineville, NC: MorningStar Publications, Inc., 1986, 1990 ed.), p. 7.

7. Edwards, Gene. *The Highest Life* (Wheaton, IL: Tyndale House, 1991).

8. Dalby, Gordon. *Father and Son—The Wound, The Healing, The Call to Manhood* (Nashville, TN: Thomas Nelson Publishers, 1992).

9. The more a person's soul [mind and emotions] is sensitive to and yielding to *spiritual* influences, (either demonic or the Holy Spirit), the *more* vulnerable that person is to *eros* love or sexual passion! This is perhaps ironic. So unless those spiritual influences are constrained by the indwelling Holy Spirit of Christ Jesus, sexual sins, distortion, and deviances are very apt to result. A very close link exists between *eros* love or *sexual* passion on one hand, and *spiritual* influences on the other. Thus sexually deviant practices (heterosexual sins, homosexuality, monosexuality [masturbation], and psychopathic sadism) are not only prevalent among satan worshipers and New Agers, but also (to the shock of many) are frequent among "spiritual" *Christians.*

10. Murray, Andrew. *The Spirit of Christ,* pp. 193-194. Copyright © 1979, Bethany Fellowship, Inc.

Chapter Two

Foundations of Spiritual Servanthood

How do we actually function in love-motivated and Spirit-empowered servanthood, especially in our marriage relationships? Most of us are far from love-motivated servanthood today because sin still deeply penetrates our natures.

Our lives reveal an important contrast between two entirely contradictory facts: We come to God in a condition of utter and total depravity; and we come with a tremendous and highly valued potential for the fulfillment of His purposes.

Both of these extremes are a shock to the typical Christian believer. Very few of us are aware of the totality of the intrinsic depravity of our "self," of our "pseudo-Christian" culture, and of our Christian traditions! But, also, very few of us understand the value God places on us—we could say He *measures our value* by the very life of His Son! The first truth keeps us humble, and the second truth encourages us with hope.

1. We Have Lost Sight of Our Utter Depravity

Evangelical Christianity largely lost sight of the depth of man's depravity during the mid-nineteenth century "backlash" against the extremes of Puritanism in America and Great Britain. It turned away from the Puritan emphasis on the depth of the human sin nature and the holiness and sovereignty of God, and its strong demands of legalistic holiness. Puritanism had presented a harsh, stark, and depressing form of Christianity. The Quakers, and later the Pentecostal movements, emphasized the inworking of the Holy Spirit, but they also demanded legalistic holiness.

Evangelicalism rose out of the wake of the Second Great Awakening and the spread of Methodism as a countermovement emphasizing the positive aspect of salvation by Christ on Calvary. Then the pendulum swung to the opposite extreme and de-emphasized both the totality of human depravity and the holiness and sovereignty of God. As a result, most evangelical Christians today fail to fully appreciate the depth of the sin nature remaining in them, and they are frustrated because they continue to try to live the life of Christ's righteousness by their *own strength* (i.e., in legalism).

Man As Fallen

Every human being since Adam who has reached an age of "accountability"[1] has sinned, has chosen the *life of self-seeking* by will or by default! (See Romans 3:23; 5:12.) That is, everyone except for one person: Christ Jesus.

This sin nature is traced to Adam and Eve's sin, and to the "Adamic curse" in Genesis 3:16-19 and 3:24. After their sin, they were denied access to the tree of life and the garden of Eden; and they inherited sorrow, work, mortality (death), and discord. This is the foundation for Romans 6:23a, which says, "For the wages [consequences that we inevitably reap] of sin is death."

Because man chose the path of *self-seeking*, God introduced physical death for the first time and forced man to struggle *on his own* simply for physical existence. Most significantly, God separated mankind from the tree (readily available source) of His life of goodness, righteousness, and love (see Gen. 3:22-24).

God imposed these consequences of the fall for our protection, though this may be difficult for us to understand (see Gen. 3:22). Even in a fallen state, man still has tremendous spiritual capabilities that satan is anxious to exploit. God forced a way of life on His "self-seeking" creation that makes it very difficult for man to deploy those spiritual capabilities.

The utter hopelessness of our state outside of Christ is described in Ephesians 2. The apostle Paul balances this harsh truth with the greater truth that Christ, by His shed blood, has purchased us from our former slave owner, satan. This means we *are still slaves*. First we served satan, now we serve Christ. We deceive ourselves if we think we can run our own lives—we can only choose our individual slave owner: satan or Christ.

At the same time, Paul wrote much about "freedom" in Romans 8:2 and Galatians 5:1. What was he talking about? Paul taught that there were two forms of "freedom": (a) freedom *from* the power of sin in our lives (and from our former slave owner, satan); and (b) freedom *to* live in fellowship with our Eternal Father as He intended, as part of the eternal Sonship of Christ Jesus (see Eph. 1:4-5,9-12).

We have a powerful enemy who constantly works against our choice to let Christ live and work in us. Our greatest enemy is not satan (although he always seeks to deceive us and exploit our weaknesses)—it is our own "self." Our "self" constantly seeks—*on its own*—to satisfy our driving self-needs. Our dark nature (apart from God) *has a power of its own,* but we normally do not realize it because of the added deception provided by satan.

A serious error is our insistence that we can live the Christian life by our own efforts. Oh no, we cannot! The principle that brings victory over "self" is this: It is utterly and completely impossible for "self" to "live" the life of Christ! Only by choosing to die to self may we experience Christ's indwelling life. Edwards makes this emphasis in his excellent book *The Secret to the Christian Life* as well.[2]

The way we learn and apply this fundamental law of life by Christ's indwelling is almost always slow and painful, but each of us must endure the process. The problem lies not so much in our deliberate rebellion as in the extremely insidious nature of our "self." This dark nature stubbornly insists on trying to "live the righteousness of Christ Jesus" *by the power of self,* though it is doomed to fail. This painful learning process is evident in the lives of every godly leader in the Bible.

The one aspect of our fallen nature most engulfed in darkness is our *intellect.* We must exercise strong mental discipline to keep our minds focused on the Lord Christ Jesus. What is the role of satan in all of this? Satan is not the *source* of the evil of "self." Man's fallen nature has *its own evil* because it "left its first estate" as God's highest creation, and was separated from God. Through the fall of Adam and Eve, satan[3] gained a "legal right" to "take over," and he is a hard and cruel slaveholder and taskmaster who acts as God's agent to enforce the Adamic curse.

Man As Being Redeemed

Through Christ, we have God's life of love (tree of life) available to us once again by faith. Before Christ's atoning death, God preserved a remnant of mankind under the "protective custody" of the Mosaic Law (see Gal. 3:21-25). Unfortunately, the vast majority of Bible-believing Christians are *still living under the Old Testament* covenant relationship with God based on the law. The original version viewed Calvary futuristically; the "new improved Christian" version views Calvary "historically." In both cases, however, salvation is sought through "good works" done by man *under the power of self.*

Now we know that our salvation is not of our own efforts, and we know it is readily available to everyone; but we still have difficulty living the Christ-life in our activities and our marriages.

2. Salvation—The End Result

What does "salvation" really mean? Putting aside the usual religious jargon and clichés, the answer may be found in the original language of the Scriptures. For instance, "salvation" in the Old Testament Hebrew (*YShIaH* and *YShI*), and the New Testament Greek (*soteria*), means to "preserve life from perishing."

What would cause our life to perish? Christians who have biblical "salvation" through Christ still experience natural death, so the Scriptures are not talking about physical death (though we will regain *physical immortality* [see 1 Cor. 15:51-56; Phil. 3:21]). Nor is "salvation" limited to "getting to Heaven after we die." It includes becoming "complete in Christ," being "conformed to His image," and ruling and reigning with Him throughout eternity (see Eph. 1:18-23; Rom. 8:29). In the same way, the "Kingdom of God" does not merely refer to Heaven after death, but Christ being King and Lord in our lives— *here* as well as *there, now* as well as *then.*

The process of salvation nullifies the Adamic curse that ensnares us. We are rescued from the Adamic curse!

Salvation is a multi-stage *process*, not a single event. Although the process begins with one life-changing encounter with the living Christ, our salvation or "preservation" from the Adamic curse involves three different tenses or "times" related to our tripartite nature. First, I *have been saved* through the actions of Christ Jesus in the past (see Eph. 2:5,8-13; 2 Tim. 1:9; Tit. 3:5). Second, I *am being saved* through a process right now, in my daily life on this earth (see 1 Cor. 15:2; Phil. 2:12). Third, I *shall be saved* through a future event if I "endure until then" (see Mt. 10:22; 24:13; Mk. 13:13, Rom. 5:9-10).

The first stage occurred when I first acknowledged Christ Jesus as my Savior and Lord, and was regenerated. The second stage is the ongoing sanctification process I am experiencing, and will continue to experience all my life. The third stage will occur when I receive my immortality as described in Philippians 3:20-21.

The first stage of salvation is sometimes called an "outward stage," since it focuses on the historical Calvary and our initial choice to have Christ Jesus rule our lives as Lord. It is our first point of contact with God's destiny for us. It introduces us into a new mentality (from the Greek word, *naos*).

In the second stage, called "sanctification," our *soul* learns how to actually *live* God's eternal life by releasing the indwelling Holy Spirit of Christ Jesus. Although the concept that "another Person" actually lives within us is foreign to our thinking at first, we are not to remain in that "outward" stage! We now have the *capacity* to release God's life through Christ's indwelling. But *our understanding* is limited to the historical, physical Christ on

Calvary. However, by continually yielding to the inward workings of the indwelling Holy Spirit of Christ Jesus through prayer, praise, worship, and study of the written Word of God, we also become increasingly aware of the reality of Christ indwelling, and learn how to release Him.

3. Learning to Live by Eternal Life

Most of us testify to a personal experience of being "born again" and of receiving "eternal life." What do those things really mean? Birth (of any kind) describes an event whereupon something or someone begins to *manifest life* that could not be, or was not, manifested prior to that event. When a person is "born again," he or she begins to manifest a different or additional form of life (eternal life) unknown prior to that event.

Eternal life is not simply a *quantity* of life (i.e., going on forever in time). It is a *quality* of life, a dynamic relationship (of a specific type) with God the Father and Christ Jesus the Son.

Eternal life means more than "forever in time," according to three elementary arguments. First, the souls of the damned also live forever in hell, yet they do not have "eternal life" (see 2 Thess. 1:8-9). Second, the Greek word for "eternal" (*aionion*), does not mean "forever in time," but "related or pertaining to the [present] eon or age." Eternal life literally refers to "that life which pertains to God's purposes in the [current] eon." God's purpose is "summing up all things in Christ" (Eph. 1:10). Third, Jesus defined eternal life in John 17:3 as knowing (from the Greek, *gnoskos*) God the Father and Christ the Son. This is *spiritual* knowledge of God.

The key essence of eternal life, then, is a dynamic Christ-indwelling relationship with God! It is the Holy

Spirit of Christ Jesus dwelling in our *human spirits*, enabling us to communicate with and directly manifest the nature of God Himself.

How Do We Receive It?

The first three Gospels show us *what we must do*: Change our thought patterns and seek Him. The Gospel of John reveals Jesus' divine mission to *impart eternal life* to us. The third chapter of the Gospel of John mentions eternal life as what actually happens in us when we obey His command to repent. What is often called the "born-again experience" is more accurately called the "repentance experience."

The immediate result of the "new birth" is the "delivery" of an immature (but very much alive) "baby." We are mere babies in our relationship with Christ at the moment of our regeneration (see 1 Cor. 3:1; Heb. 5:13; 1 Pet. 2:2; 1 John 2:1,12-13). Although we are immature and imperfect at "birth," we are genuine "members" of God's "household" or "family." Thus we immediately become the objects of His love, protection, and provision.

God also wants us to *grow up* in Him. From the moment of our rebirth, God begins His sanctifying process of maturation by working in us day by day and minute by minute, to deepen our understanding and dynamic personal relationship with Him.

How Do We Live It?

Eternal life only proceeds from Christ Himself living in us. This is the full meaning of "walking in faith." This is not some "mystic ability" He has given to us. His life must actually be lived dynamically, or it will lie dormant as a meaningless potential (like a baby being born in a comatose state). We must make decisive and aggressive choices to release the life of Christ in our lives to fulfill God's purposes.

How do we choose to release Christ's life? We know this: We cannot live the life of *Christ-the-Indwelling King* unless we first live the life of *Christ-the-Indwelling Lamb*! Christ, the Lamb of God, is our perfect role model for *love-motivated servanthood*. He thought, lived, and acted to fulfill God's specific purpose for Him in the earth. Spirit-empowerment follows and undergirds love-motivation in our servanthood. Christ, the Lamb of God, exhibits patience, humility, meekness, and total resignation to the ways and will of God.

This life of Christ is *not* mere doctrine *about* His life. Jesus is Life, whereas doctrine alone is the tree of knowledge. Who or what is the focal point of our attention: Jesus or intellectual understanding? Rick Joyner writes:

> Being a Christian is not just understanding certain doctrines and spiritual principles—it is having one's life in Jesus. If the truth leads us to life in Jesus, it has accomplished its purpose. But if the truth becomes the focal point, it kills....[4]

Our first step must be to *desire* and choose to live Christ's life! We must intensely *long* to be in *union* with Him!

4. What Are "Repentance" and "Faith"?

"Repentance" and "faith" are related terms. In fact, faith is a necessary element of repentance, and both are foundational to the Christian life. The Scriptures give us glimpses of the *results* of these concepts in action, rather than of the concepts themselves.

"Repent" and "believe" are actions of the will, not the mind or intellect. The Greek words *metanoeo* (a verb that means "to repent") and *metanoia* (a noun meaning "repentance") are compound words that describe a *drastic or total change in our thought patterns. Meta* means to change completely or drastically. Repentance, therefore, is far more than merely "accepting Christ as our personal Savior." It is a total yielding unto Him of the areas of darkness in our thoughts, a yielding that requires our total involvement as an act of faith.

Faith is a personal choice to respond to God in three ways: (a) by seeing Him in His spiritual reality; (b) by dynamically depending upon Him (as a Person, not just on our knowledge about Him); and (c) by sensitively obeying Him with a motivation of love. Hebrews 11:1 begins with the phrase, "Now faith is." Faith only exists or applies to the present moment. We never have to exercise faith for past events; nor even for future promises (the word *hope*, which really means "certainty," applies there).

Faith must start with an initiative by God; then we may choose to respond. The fact remains that even when the urge to believe is within us, it is still hard to trust in someone whose existence we doubt. If we wish to grow in faith, we must learn to see God and gaze upon Him. Faith is seeing Christ, choosing to utterly abandon ourselves in dynamic dependence upon Him, and sensitively obeying His revealed will.

Actually Walking in Faith

Repentance and faith do not exist as separate entities and cannot be intellectually defined. Rather, they are attributes of our personal *relationship* with Christ Jesus, and they exist only during those times when that relationship is being exercised. Furthermore, most aspects of our relationship are in *spirit* and hence require a much deeper understanding of things of *spirit* before we can more fully grasp them. They are experiences we are to *live* out of love-motivated *choice*, not doctrines for us to mentally learn. This choice makes it possible for us to begin to perceive and receive Him fully as a *spiritual* reality.

God wants us to *allow* His Holy Spirit to completely control our entire beings—to live His life in and through us as He wills, unhindered by our self-interests and desires. It is His subsequent dealings in our lives that the Bible refers to as the "baptism into the Holy Spirit" and "sanctification." Sadly, most of us are not totally yielding to His indwelling presence, even though we received the baptism into the Holy Spirit many years ago. *That is perhaps the greatest tragedy of Church history.* Our lives are not distinctive; we have all but completely adopted the ways and thinking of the world.

God's sole purpose and intention for our baptism into the Holy Spirit was that *we become Christ-centered.* He immerses our souls (our minds, emotions, and wills) into the indwelling Holy Spirit of Christ Jesus to enable us to grow in our spiritual understanding and communion with Jesus Christ. It is the beginning of a deeper and eternal relationship with our Redeemer.

5. Releasing Christ in Us

"Walking in faith" is really releasing the life of the indwelling Christ. This faith-release of His life within us involves three elements: (a) we *will* or *choose* to release His life; (b) we *declare* it being done or becoming so; and (c) we *anticipate* its completion. Perhaps our greatest stumbling block is not whether God *can* do it, but rather *will* He?

"Spirit-filled" Christians today are *spiritually impotent* because they have not yet learned to release the power of the life of the indwelling Christ. How do we release His life within us? We must desire and choose to exhibit the *virtues* of Christ as the Lamb of God, which include patience, humility, meekness, and utter resignation to the ways and will of God.

When we declare something "in faith," we are really praying and acting in His Name or agency. This walk of faith-release is something we must grow into by practicing it. Our inner awareness of faith grows through much "trial and error," and it isn't easy. This process typically goes through four stages: (a) *travail* over the burden and what God's will truly is in it; (b) *complete surrender* to God's will as we understand it; (c) a *battle* of "second thoughts" as we ward off the fiery darts of satan; and (d) *full assurance* in faith.

How do we grow in faith? Here are five key steps that describe the process:

1. *Desire Him.* In First Corinthians 14:1 Paul says, in effect, "...desire the 'spirituals' with white-hot intensity...."

2. Focus your *attention* onto Him. This involves more than mind "belief" about Him. Thank Him, praise Him, worship Him, converse with Him in prayer.

3. *Determine*, decide, and declare that He dwells within you, and that you are dead to sin and resurrected in Him. This is a matter of choice, not intellectual belief. It is the most difficult step

because our intellectual beliefs are our greatest stumbling blocks.

4. *Practice* the virtues of Christ-the-Indwelling-Lamb-of-God. This releases the power of eternal life of the indwelling Christ. William Law lists four such virtues: patience, humbleness, meekness, and total resignation to the ways and will of God.

5. *Yield* to His workings. Trials burn into our awareness the utter and total helplessness of our "self" to live His indwelling life, as well as the marvel of His living His life through us.

Dying to Self

We must die to self along with yielding to Christ's indwelling. The New Testament word for "death," *thanatos*, refers to the *effect* of dying, not the *process* of dying. The effect of dying is *separation*. Because of Christ's death on Calvary and His resurrection in us, we have the capacity of *being separated from the power of our self*. Even though we have Christ's power within us, we must *choose* to deploy it, and that is where faith really comes in.

It is not just our *sin nature* we must die to, but we must also die to "self," the "power source" for our sin-nature. This fact is lost in the prevailing teaching that we have two "natures"—the "old man" and the "new man," and that we will always have the "old man" with us while still in this life.

This is not quite true, and it confuses many Christians. *We only have one "nature."*[5] This issue between the "old man" and the "new man" is *who* rules our lives: self, or Christ? We still have the potential for the "old life" of self. However, the power of the "new life" of the indwelling Christ enables us to *live by His life* and to *be separated* from (dead to) the powers of sin and self. In other words, we can choose to live the life of Christ within us instead of the life of "self" and sin.

6. Being Purged Through Inner Heart Healing

In actual practice, this separation from self and union with the indwelling Christ is rarely a clear-cut, once-and-for-all event. For those of us who choose Christ Jesus to be our Lord, the process of purging our soul from satan's influence is not a simple or sudden accomplishment. *Sanctification* is a process that requires time! The most critical aspect of that process is our choice to *discipline* our *thought*-life so it will be continually *Christ*-oriented!

The indwelling Holy Spirit works constantly to (a) purify or "spiritualize" our faith, our gazing upon Him, our dependence upon and obedience to Him, in His spiritual reality; and to (b) purify our hearts. He brings inner heart healing to us for everything that would hinder the flow of His light, life, and love through us to others.

God isn't satisfied with our tendency to merely "visualize Christ" with our natural thinking (i.e., doctrinally). He wants to "spiritualize" our faith, so we will totally trust, depend upon, blindly obey, and abandon ourselves unto Him as a *spiritual reality*. Most of us simply refuse to do it, and we cling to our familiar "security blankets" of Christian legalism, denominationalism, and "churchianity." We understand and like these things, but "we grow not."

Most of us also refuse to embrace the inner heart healing process because it is painful, difficult, and humbling.

We simply refuse to admit our need for this healing, or we dismiss the value of the process altogether. This is most especially true in the area that most urgently needs cleansing: *the marriage relationship.* The divorce rate among "Spirit-filled" and Bible-believing Christians in America is nearly as high as the national divorce rate! Unless we get our act together, we will never be able to help others find healing, strength, and salvation in Christ! This purging work of the indwelling Holy Spirit unto our inner heart healing is so important, we devote several chapters in Part II of this book to its several aspects.

The Awesome Depth of Our Sin-Nature

The human spirit-soul combination has a virtually unlimited capacity for evil in its fallen state apart from God. The unlimited nature of this capacity, and the depth of deception that has enslaved us, are astounding. *By working through the human spirit, the soul has an unlimited potential for two-way communication with the entire "spirit" world!* At the same time, the soul can also use the "flesh" to interact with the physical world. In addition to these incredible abilities, the soul also has the full potential for logical thought and free choice. What remarkable creatures we are, made but a "little lower than the angels [Godhead]" (see Ps. 8:5; Heb. 2:7)!

God will only restore the full ability of our souls to communicate spiritually with Him *after* we choose *full oneness* with Him. This restoration takes place through a step-by-step process after we become "born again" or regenerated through Christ. *Mature* Spirit-filled believers "have the mind of Christ," but most Christians are not yet mature. More accurately, we possess the mind of Christ only to the extent to which we are mature. In reality, most of the things that we think are "of the Spirit" are actually products and perceptions of our own souls!

The *psuche* or soul requires supernatural (spiritual) power for its full development, so it tends to be governed and empowered by one or more of three forces: (a) the animal drives (flesh) of the body; (b) the Holy Spirit of Christ Jesus through our human spirits; or (c) the latent spirit-soul powers activated by spiritual forces other than God (i.e., by satan).

Since the fall of man, most of the power used for his soulish development has come from satan rather than from God. We are caught in a continual warfare between the powerful and totally conflicting forces of a supreme God and His defeated foe, satan. Although satan cannot hope to escape his bitter end, he knows that God seeks children who come to Him in love by choice. Satan eagerly and desperately seeks to hinder God's purposes and steal, kill, or destroy His prized creation, man. *Our spirit-soul combination is both the battleground and the prize of that war.* God *draws* us by His love, power, and Word, ever leading us to *choose* to yield to Him; while satan *ensnares* us through simple *lusts* of the flesh, through *religion* and through *supernatural* influences such as the occult.

One of our most overlooked "latent spirit-soul powers" is the spiritual influence of our *thoughts* (even when not audibly spoken). Our thoughts, good and bad, prayerful and mundane, all *radiate* into the spiritual world about us! We call this radiating or projecting of our thoughts into the spiritual world "soul-power" or "soul-force." (E.S.P. is a satanic exploitation of this "latent spirit-soul power" to enslave "scientific" people.)

Even our mundane thoughts can, and do, hinder the Holy Spirit's work in others near us, such as in church during corporate worship. This applies to more than just our sinful thoughts; it includes all of our anxieties, dreams, and worldly concerns. This is particularly true of our prayers, which can exert a definite influence on others through our "soul-powers," *even outside of God's will*! Our "spiritual fragrance" is a "spiritual aura" about us, discernible by God, by the Holy Spirit, and even by evil spirits.

We also misuse the "soul-power" of our minds to try to "figure out" the ways of God so we can "build His Kingdom for Him." There is a big difference between our doing things (as we determine them) for Him, and *yielding to Him in us*, doing things (as He determines) through us! Andrew Murray issued a strong warning to the Church about the soul:

> The greatest danger the religion of the Church or the individual has to dread is the inordinate activity of the soul, with its power of mind and will. ...Many a believer has no conception of the reality of the Spirit's indwelling, and of the extent to which He must get the mastery of the soul, that is, of our whole self in all our feelings and thinking and willing, so as to purge out all confidence in the flesh, and work that teachableness and submissiveness which is indispensable to the Spirit's doing His work.[6]

Jesse Penn-Lewis noted: "...even when a man becomes regenerate, and has the life of God in his spirit, through ignorance he may be using soul-force, even in his mission work for God."[7]

The soul also has a dangerous ability and tendency to *counterfeit* that which is truly spiritual. Every work of the Holy Spirit of Christ Jesus (except *agape* love) can be (and has been) counterfeited through "soul-force" in believers who are under the subtle activation of satan.

This counterfeiting ability of the soul often appears in our *worship*. We often substitute mere religious praise for worship, believing that we are thereby in His presence. Jesse Penn-Lewis asks a disturbing question:

> "God is a Spirit, and they that worship Him must worship Him in spirit and in truth." ...some people, living a worldly life all the week, become so happy because they have gone to church on Sunday. ...through the music and other influences, they have been made happy and comforted. They have been soothed, but the question is, have they been truly convicted of sin and [been] regenerated?[8]

Sanctification of Our Triparte Nature by Emptying Trials

Sanctify means "to separate from profane things" and "to purify." As the Lord draws us toward maturity in Him, all three aspects of our psychological nature must be dealt with. God deals with these aspects separately and in totally different ways. The apostle Paul reveals an order or time-sequence for our *sanctification* in First Thessalonians 5:23: "Now may the God of peace Himself sanctify you entirely; and may your *spirit* and *soul* and *body* be preserved complete, without blame at the coming of our Lord Jesus Christ."

The human *spirit* is "sanctified" first upon regeneration. This is a one-time "crisis" event in our lives, although we may not be consciously aware of it at the time.[9] Next, the human *soul* is sanctified as we increasingly yield our soul-functions (of the mind, the emotions, and the will) to the Holy Spirit, who already indwells our spirits. At this stage, we become experientially aware of the Holy Spirit, who has already been dwelling in us. Finally, our bodies are sanctified upon final redemption in conjunction with Christ's return when we become established fully in Him. Our carnality (*sarx*) can never be sanctified; it must be reckoned as crucified; it must die! In fact, we progress in our soul-sanctification to the extent that we reckon our *sarx* dead!

The human soul is the most difficult of the three aspects of the human psychological structure to fully yield to the lordship of Jesus Christ. It is the seat of the "self," the great "I", the Adamic nature. No matter how strongly we desire (and pray) to be yielded to the Lord, the soul will continue to dominate our behavior and to suppress the human spirit until the soul determines to yield.

Our minds demand understanding; our wills demand that understanding precede commitment; and our emotions confuse and deceive us. Nevertheless, the Lord has chosen to never force us into anything against our wills. Thus, He draws us unto entire soul-sanctification through a combination of: (a) loving enticements by His love (to soften our emotions); (b) physical miracles that our minds cannot understand, such as tongues, healings, and victories over our passions (to weaken our minds; dominance); and (c) trials and tribulations in the circumstances of our daily lives (to redirect our wills).

7. The Bottom Line: Love-Motivated and Spirit-Empowered Servanthood

As engrafted members of the Godhead, we are created to "live to serve others," to live primarily for the best interests of others. We were created for servanthood! Jesus Christ wants to manifest Himself *through us* as suffering servant, priest, savior, healer, deliverer, teacher, and prophet. He *lives in and through us* to heal the broken-hearted, to set the captives free, to mature His Bride. God dwells within us to manifest His love to others through dynamic, responsible, aggressive servanthood.

The ministry of our *supernatural Savior* through our lives requires *supernatural* wisdom and power. He alone can love others in a full sense. He alone can be the High Priest between mankind and God. He alone can save, heal, and deliver. We must yield to His will and allow His power to do all things through *Spirit empowerment* in our love-motivated servanthood! We can only be fulfilled in our destiny to be a vessel of Christ on earth by living at the level of dynamic spiritual power that the Bible clearly states is physically possible. Sadly, this is far beyond the actual experiences of most Christians today, even Bible-believing, "Spirit-filled" Christians. Obviously we have much to learn.

End Notes: Chapter Two

1. The "age of accountability" is a time, determined solely by God, at which a person becomes capable of choosing to accept or reject God's Way of Life. It *varies considerably* between individuals; therefore, *it is not some specific age* (such as 3 days or 11 years) to be established by church doctrine or any other institution or individual.

2. Edwards, Gene. *The Secret to the Christian Life* (Beaumont, TX: The Seed Sowers, 1991).

3. To be sure, satan has objectives of his own. If we are unredeemed, we are his. A life of "total self-seeking" passes through death to become hell—literally as well as figuratively. If satan can entice men into a *spiritual* life of self-seeking while still in this physical life, then they become powerful tools he can use to impose his will in the physical world. How many wars and atrocities have been instigated by people dominated by the spirit and purposes of satan?

4. Joyner, Rick. *There Were Two Trees In The Garden* (Pineville, NC: MorningStar Publications, Inc., 1986, 1990 ed.), p. 34.

5. Our human nature consists of a physical body, plus a human spirit, plus a soul, plus physical senses.

6. Murray, Andrew. *The Spirit of Christ* (Minneapolis, MN: Bethany Fellowship, Inc., 1979), p. 229. Copyright © 1979 by Bethany Fellowship, Inc.

7. Penn-Lewis, Jesse. *Soul and Spirit* (Fort Washington, PA: Christian Literature Crusade, 8th edition, 1965), p. 65.

8. Penn-Lewis. *Soul and Spirit*, p. 75.

9. In my personal experience, more than six years passed before I finally began to understand what had actually happened.

Chapter Three

Harmony in Human Sexuality

And God created man in His own image, in the image of God He created him; male and female He created them (Genesis 1:27).

Human sexuality is our greatest area of weakness. It is here that satan's attacks have the highest probability of ultimately destroying us. Most of us are inwardly baffled and frustrated by our sexuality, since the biblical truths about sexuality seem so contrary to our personal experiences, intense feelings, and secular culture.

Unmarried Christians are overwhelmed in their struggles with the hedonistic promiscuity of our world. At the same time, virtually every Christian married couple I am acquainted with is beset with well-hidden but heart-rending hurts, disappointments, loneliness, and contention. Many Christian marriages seem to be "stalemated" at best.

More than 20 years ago, Norman Grubb expressed both the frustration and the hope of Christian marriage:

Sex problems...about which we evangelicals have been so hush-hush, are often a cause of frustration within the married life and without; and frank talking leading to a healthier understanding and adjustment is often the key to a new release....

...If pleasure replaces purpose as the end in itself, that is corruption leading to hell. If purpose is out front, then pleasure is a happy companion. ... If sex is for self-gratification, the end is death, as Proverbs makes emphatically clear [Chapters 2, 5, 6, 7, and 9]. If in the marriage bond it is a token of the total self-giving of the one to the other, then it has the fulfillment Proverbs [Chapter 5] also speaks of.

...[*Eros*] love is the human means for the expression of God loving by us, our passions are the channel for His compassion... . We dare to understand ourselves, accept ourselves and give ourselves in human relationships—to love with His love, responding to that hunger in all to be loved and to love, till...[he/she] find in us, not one human loving another, but Christ loving...[him/her] through a human love.[1]

The confusion Christians feel over how they view human sexuality stems from two main sources: (a) the heavy and distorted emphasis given by psychologists to the sex drives *as the essence of masculinity and femininity*; and (b) the shame we all feel concerning our sexuality due to the Fall.

1. Sexuality for Christian Servanthood?

God created us male and female for the purpose of servanthood! Our masculinity and femininity equip us for that servanthood in ways that go far beyond our physiological attributes. Servanthood is an all-encompassing paradigm, a way of thinking, a view of life; it is the essence of purpose and goals in life. It is for servanthood that God knew Adam needed a "help meet." It contains concepts of "headship" and "submission" that are far from "command" and "obey." They are forms of God-intended servanthood unique to our sexuality paradigm.

God originally created us to live according to the "Tree Of Life," ever functioning to serve the needs of *others*, never seeking by our own efforts to have our own needs served. *It is in that context that human sexuality makes marvelous sense.* It is difficult for most of us to grasp the fact that Christ Jesus wants to *express Himself* (His acceptance and love) to our spouses through our human sexuality! But that is one aspect of His expression. It provides an immediate, tangible way for us to feel and to experience His love. Yet even in the most harmonious of Christian marriages, few of us ever experience the deep richness of sexuality *as an expression of Christ's love* for and through our spouses!

Dr. Larry Crabb distills all of our social, psychological, moral, and spiritual responsibilities as men and women down to one thing: love-motivated servanthood.

Understanding masculinity and femininity begins with learning what another person needs with the intent of supplying that need if we can. ... The more a man understands a woman and is controlled by a Spirit-prompted other-centered commitment to bless her, the more "masculine" he becomes. ... In exactly the same way, the more a woman understands a man and is preoccupied with doing all she can for him, the more "feminine" she naturally becomes. We will neither understand nor enjoy our sexual natures until we take seriously our responsibility to use our distinct natures to serve others.[2]

2. From Curse to Christ

Human sexuality, explained in physiological terms *apart from the implications of the Fall,* totally misses the main points. God's order for the husband-wife relationship (both before and after the Fall) is one of the most widely misunderstood truths among Christians today.

Adam and Eve were mature, complete adults who were created *equal* yet *different.* Adam, the human male, tended to concentrate on "physical things and facts" apart from immediate human needs. Eve, the human female, however, was particularly sensitive to human social needs. She was concerned with the practical needs of bearing children and *maturing them.*

As part of the Adamic curse, God established *husband-wife tensions* to "protect" and preserve the human family unit *outside of fellowship with God!*

How did this work? Examine God's description of the husband-wife relationship *after* the Fall in Genesis 3:16b: "Yet your *desire* shall be for your husband, and [but] he shall *rule* over you."

"Desire" (*TsHWQaH*) is a Hebrew word that literally means "clutch to possess." The sense here is that the wife will continually strive to manipulate, control, and dominate her husband for personal satisfaction, in the same sense as a lion "clutching" its prey. The Hebrew word translated as "rule" is *MShL,* which means "to rule or dominate with power and authority" as a king rules his subjects, or a master rules his slaves.

This makes for an explosive situation as each sex, with the intrinsic nature to seek domination and control over the other, strives for the upper hand: she with her prowess, wile, and social wisdom; and he with his logic and physical force. That is a good definition of tension! (It is also the definition of marriage, christian or not, apart from God-empowered, love-motivated servanthood.)

God waited 4,000 years for the resurrection of Christ Jesus to undo the Adamic curse and restore the relationship of cooperative harmony to human marriages. If the sexes were not so obsessed with dominating each other, no marriage outside of the lordship of Christ Jesus would have survived. Men and women are so different in their ways of thinking that without such obsessions, they could never tolerate each other for more than a few years at most. This would result in total family breakdown and its social chaos. That is exactly what is happening across the world today. There is an unprecedented rise in homosexuality and lesbianism as the sexes are increasingly remaining independent and failing to find their true identities as men and women.

Contrast this tension under the Adamic curse with God's ordained order of the husband-wife relationship *in Christ* (see Eph. 5:22-25; Col. 3:12-19; 1 Pet. 3:1-2,7-9). The husband is to *agape* (self-sacrificially love) his wife as Christ *agape*-loves us, not dominate her. The wife is to *upotasso* (be in harmonious rapport with) her husband as we are with Christ, not strive to manipulate and control him. *Both partners* are to *take the initiative*: He is to love her; and she is to respond to him. This is a *major* change in our marriage relationship from the tension of the curse to the servanthood in Christ. It does not occur upon regeneration; it is a life-long process involving change, struggle, total commitment, and yielding to the Spirit of Christ within us.

3. Harmony in Human Sexuality?

What are the biblical, practical concepts of masculinity and femininity? The answer begins with what sexuality is *not.* The *essence* of human sexuality is *not* sexual intercourse. It is the social, psychological, moral, and spiritual responsibilities associated with it.

George Alan Rekers makes that point quite emphatically:

> The popular Playboy platitudes...falsely preach that the most masculine attribute is unrestrained intercourse. This irresponsible attitude pretends that we can isolate biological masculinity from social or moral aspects of the male role. ... As a whole person, the man's role involves social responsibilities of father and husband.... Similarly, a true female sexual identity involves the whole person in her biological, psychological, social, and spiritual life.[3]

Sexuality Is a Paradigm

Human sexuality is first and foremost a *paradigm* or a framework of thinking; its physiological attributes are secondary. It reflects the particular relationship God intends for husbands and wives to share as they each allow the indwelling Christ to bring their loved ones more fully unto Him. Our struggles with sexuality do not stem from mere bodily urges or carnal ways of thinking—our problems stem from our *separation from God.*

Dr. Crabb noted:

> The uniqueness of being male or female reaches to the very core of our identity. ... Everything a man does, he does as a man. Everything a woman does, she does as a woman.
>
> Men were designed to enter their worlds strongly, providing for their families, leading them (through servanthood) toward God, moving toward others

with sacrificing, powerful love. Women were designed to courageously give all they have (intellect, talents, wisdom, kindness, etc.) to others in warm vulnerability, allowing themselves to be entered and wrapping themselves with supportive strength around those with whom they relate, offering all they are as female image-bearers [of Christ] for a godly purpose.[4]

Different in Responsibilities and Needs

The differences between Eve and Adam are not just physical; they are *psychological* (in the human spirit and soul) as well. The human male tends to concentrate on logic and deals with physical "things" and facts, to accomplish tasks and solve problems apart from immediate human needs. Men are usually less sensitive than women to the subtle needs of people, of children, and the innuendoes of social interactions. Men are generally more sensitive to impersonal facts and logic, and they have a very strong drive to seek physical and logical completeness—even at the expense of human emotional needs. It is particularly hard for the male to augment his forthrightness with Christ's command to love other people.

God created women with tremendous powers to influence people. They are particularly sensitive to social needs, and the practical needs of not only *bearing* children but *maturing* them. This is why a woman can exert such powerful psychological influence on other people by deploying her natural "wile." Women have an especially powerful gift of intuition (particularly pertaining to human needs). It is often difficult for women to align themselves with directions from the Lord because these sometimes run counter to the human needs that they sense through their soulish intuition.

The male obviously possesses some of the psychological characteristics of the female, but on a much smaller scale of intensity. In the same way, the female also possesses some of the psychological characteristics of the male, but again, on a much smaller scale of intensity. However, these are primary differences between the relative weaknesses and strengths of men and women.

Other non-reproductive differences between male and female are many. Men generally experience more quick, intense feelings than women, who tend to feel strong emotions over longer periods of time than men. Although men respond quickly to external visual stimuli, women tend to respond more deeply to touch and external audible stimuli. Men seem to hear low frequency sounds more keenly than women, but women score higher with high frequency sounds, etc.

Even the Hebrew and Greek languages typify the differences between men and women. All the words pertaining to God and to the human spirit are masculine in gender, while words pertaining to human situations and the human soul are feminine in gender.

Dynamic Teamwork by Rapport

God ordained men and women to be *different* in function, purpose, and mentality, but of *equal value/worth* in relationship with Him. Adam was complete in his walk with God. Eve, apart from Adam, was also complete in her walk with God and her fellowship with Him. Thus God had another purpose in mind when He created them. In Genesis 1:28, God said to both Adam and Eve, in effect, "You [plural in the Hebrew: the two of you together] be fruitful and multiply, and fill the earth, and subdue it."

The phrase "be fruitful and multiply" is qualitative, not quantitative! "To multiply" means "to reproduce like kind." That means spiritually as well as physically, since we were created in God's image. It means to reproduce "Adams and Eves" *as they were at that time*—not just *immature* children, but people who also are *complete* in their relationship with God. That can only be done as we release the indwelling Christ to minister His love, acceptance, and significance through us into each other!

God declared that Adam needed a "help meet" (*ITZR KNGDW*) in Genesis 2:18-24. *ITZR* means "helper or ally or completion," as needed to accomplish a specific task. *KNGDW* has the meaning of "corresponding," just as two adjacent pieces of a jigsaw puzzle fit together, but in a dynamic sense. A similar New Testament Greek word, *upotasso* (usually translated as "submission" or "being subject to"), actually means *"to be properly dynamically related to in rapport and harmony."*

God created man and woman to be different from each other and yet complementary, in the sense that where he's weak, she's strong, and where she's weak, he's strong. Eve wasn't created to make Adam a better man to multiply. God wanted "Adam plus Eve," working together as a coordinating unit, to multiply and nurture more "mature and complete Christians."[5]

Husbands and wives are to function as a team. At least three conditions must exist for them, as a team, to fulfill their calling. *Each partner must*:

1. Focus on and be totally committed to *their common goal* of "reproducing mature Christians."

2. Fully *deploy and operate* in every skill, calling, or ability unique to each.

3. Truly *care for* his or her spouse with genuine compassion, and seek the best interests of the other.

Release Your Partner to Be All God Intends

The biblical admonitions for husbands to *love* their wives, and for wives to *submit* to their husbands, are not intended to be legalistic constraints. They were given to encourage each partner to live according to this God-ordained paradigm of sexuality, so that each is released to fulfill God's calling in Christ. The issues here are *release* and *freedom*, not constraint and bondage.

Man's God-ordained paradigm is his *authority* and the fruit of his *labor/accomplishments* to provide his loved ones with protection, security, and nourishment (physical, economic, emotional, and spiritual).

Women serve their loved ones by *being* a constant, intimate source of nurture, comfort, encouragement, and harmony. She serves by *giving herself* as a nurturer and encourager according to her God-ordained paradigm. When she truly serves in her unique way, her loved ones (particularly her husband) are strengthened and encouraged to focus completely on their (his) means of servanthood.

We must also remember that both marriage partners share a deep need for their spouse to *receive* their "giving." This is a deep aspect of human sexuality.

A wife needs one thing from her husband more than economic and physical security: She needs him to *fully accept her as the person she is* and genuinely appreciate her as an intrinsically precious and worthy person. This acceptance must be given freely—regardless of what he receives from her. This attitude must be consistently expressed by the commitment to spend much effective time with her as a compassionate friend. *The one thing that a wife detests most* from her husband is the sense of *being used* by him for his *selfish desires*.

A husband needs one thing from his wife more than sex and good cooking! He desperately needs her to *respect him for the person he is,* and encourage him in his striving to be the God-ordained head of the family (in the servanthood sense of providing and caring, etc.). This attitude must be consistently expressed through her warm reception of his servanthood to her. *The one thing a husband detests most* from his wife is the sense that she rejects his servanthood to her, and does not think he is capable of meeting his responsibilities properly without her *intervention.*

By serving each other according to God's intention, we are released from the driving need to find fulfillment for "self." Vast amounts of time and energy formerly spent in self-seeking are released for the deeply satisfying functions God created us for in the first place! But if one or both partners fail to assume their proper responsibilities, then the strain on their relationship and marriage can become overwhelming.

4. Husbands and Wives as Christ and His Bride

And be subject to one another in the fear of Christ. Wives, be subject to your own husbands, as to the Lord. For the husband is the head of the wife, as Christ also is the head of the church, He Himself being the Savior of the body. But as the church is subject to Christ, so also the wives ought to be to their husbands in everything. Husbands, love your wives, just as Christ also loved the church and gave Himself up for her; that He might sanctify her... (Ephesians 5:21-26).

Wives, be subject to your husbands, as is fitting in the Lord. Husbands, love [agapao] *your wives, and do not be embittered against them* (Colossians 3:18-19).

...wives, be submissive to your own husbands so that even if any of them are disobedient to the word, they may be won without a word by the behavior of their wives, as they observe your chaste and respectful behavior. ... You husbands likewise, live with your wives in an understanding way...grant her honor as a fellow heir of the grace of life, so that your prayers may not be hindered (1 Peter 3:1-2,7).

Notice the comparison between the marriage relationship and the relationship the Lord desires to have with His church. Paul uses the comparison to help us understand how our Christian *marriages* are to work—not to help us understand the Christ-church relationship. His first century readers had a much deeper experiential knowledge of that than we do today.

The word for "head" or "headship" in Ephesians 5:22-26 is *kephale*, which has the meaning of "covering" with protection and provision. The husband is to treat his wife *exactly as Christ treats us, His Body and Bride.* That's a far cry from issuing commands and orders from some central command center. In the footsteps of Christ Jesus, the husband is authorized and responsible to provide forgiveness, mercy, understanding, protection, provision, encouragement, and compassion. That's *real* masculinity!

The word for "submission" in Ephesians 5 (the noun, *upotassetai,* and the verb *upotasso*) means the wife is to respond to her husband *exactly as we respond to Christ.* That's a far cry from "blind obedience" to every command, or manipulative disregard and disrespect! The woman takes most of the initiatives to "dynamically interact with her husband in harmonious rapport" (the accurate meaning of *upotassetai*). That is *real* femininity!

Actually each partner in a marriage relationship is to *upotasso* and *agapao* the other! However, they need these different *emphases* in admonitions to become complete in their relationship in Christ. God *commanded* men to *love* and women to *submit* because of the particular weaknesses inherent in each sex, in order to provide protection where their tendencies under the Adamic curse fall short. A woman's tremendous power to influence other people often makes it harder for her to *upotasso* (submit to) her husband than to *agapao* (love) him. God commands that she submit. A man in general is particularly vulnerable to having negative reactions borne out of his frustration over his wife's demands upon him, coupled with his inability to understand her. This makes it harder for a husband to *agapao* (love) his wife, than to *upotasso* (submit or align with) her. God commands that he love.

Wives, Respect Your Husbands!

Again, *upotasso*, the Greek word translated as "submit," literally means, "to properly order one's interpersonal relationships with another person." Actual application varies with the degree of rapport and the context of the individuals. The marriage relationship requires a high level of rapport. Again *upotasso*, as practiced within marriage, specially refers to "being in harmonious rapport with, being properly ordered in personal relationship with, closely cooperating with and mutually supporting each other, and each doing what the other does less efficiently."

Thus, *upotasso* in the writings of Paul and Peter constitutes a command for a wife to put herself in close order with her husband—in oneness with him. It means to be in correspondence with, to be in oneness with (as Eve was created to be with Adam); to complete the family unit, and *to be restored from the Adamic curse* to God's original purpose for her with her husband.

It is vital to see that the first woman came under the first man's rule *solely* by the Adamic curse. That was due to the second part of the curse, where God told her "your *desire* shall be for your husband" (Gen. 3:16). Eve acquired a new "natural tendency," a desire (*TShWQaH*) to continually "clutch" on to, manipulate, control, and dominate her husband. Both extremes—Eve's tendency and Adam's ruling domination—were not part of God's original creation, but a *consequence of the Adamic curse.*

But Christ Jesus *nullifies* the Adamic curse! Galatians 3:28 declares, "...there is neither male nor female; for you are all one in Christ Jesus." This passage refers to both our *ultimate* role with Christ, and that toward which God is adjusting in us here and now.

If Christ Jesus has nullified the Adamic curse over a woman, then is she *secondary* to her husband? Is she bound to *blindly obey* his every command like a slave or robot? No. The New Testament commands apply *to the extent that each partner truly yields to Christ Jesus* as He nullifies the Adamic curse in their daily lives and practical relationship. *To the extent that it is not the case*, then perhaps they should interpret "subject" legalistically (as "obey"). This at least restores the Old Testament balance of tension to their marriage relationship, and helps them avoid being destroyed by sin and the forces of the world (see Galatians 3:23).

What does a Christian wife have to do to come into "harmonious rapport" with her husband? To *upotasso* literally means to become totally one with him in attitudes, thoughts, will, finances, discipline of children, and family goals. It is far more difficult for a wife to *upotasso* (become totally one with) her husband than it is to simply obey him or to minister to his fleshly needs. Simple obedience requires neither love nor respect.

Husbands (both saved and unsaved) are crying out in silent desperation for their wives to simply *respect* and *appreciate* them. Wives hurt their husbands in ways far deeper than they realize when they fail to respect their husbands in their attitudes! God commands that every wife's attitudes become Christlike.

This conflicts strongly with the socially matriarchal role of the wife in the family. This destructive role has been inbred in all of us by our American culture and life style, with its European and Mediterranean origins. Will we choose God's better way?

The wife of a respected church elder has written some excellent insights into the relationship of a woman to her husband in Christ:

> ...the most important quality to be found in an Elder's wife is that she be deeply in love with her husband.... It is as a result of her love and trust-relationship with the Beloved Bridegroom of the Church, that she increasingly learns how to love her Earthly bridegroom...
>
> ... By nature we are very insecure creatures. We long for security and acceptance. Any relationship in which we seek to draw from another human our main source of security and acceptance will become strained and disappointing.[6]

Husbands, Love Your Wives!

How about Christian husbands—what are they commanded to do? "Husbands, love your wives, and do not be embittered against them" (Col. 3:19).

The original language of this passage is Greek. There are four different Greek words translated as "love" with entirely different meanings. *Eros* describes passionate or sexual love; *phileo* describes the love of friends who share common interests; *storge*[7] is used to describe the love of security in a family sense. None of these words are used in Colossians 3:19. This Scripture uses the Greek word *agapao*.

Agapao has almost nothing to do with feelings; it is a command of the human will. We may or may not feel or even want it, but we *choose* it by an act of will. True *agapao* love motivates us to do everything we can for the benefit of another person—even unto death. *Agapao* is total self-sacrificing love without any expectation of receiving anything in return. It is love given solely for his or her benefit; it consists of love-acts of the will, not matters of mere feeling or emotion.

No husband can *agapao* (sacrificially love) his wife until he has Christ indwelling. Even then, this love flows *only as he yields* to the indwelling Christ. Yet this is the very kind of love that wives need the most! Wives (both saved and unsaved) are *desperately* crying out for their husbands simply to love them, to care about and accept them *for who they are* (not merely for what she *does* for him). They are hurt in ways far deeper than their husbands realize when these men fail to truly *agapao* (sacrificially love) their wives! God commands that every husband's attitudes become Christlike.

The same elder's wife quoted earlier provides a particularly crucial warning to men involved in ministry:

The greatest necessity in a woman's life...is that she be deeply loved by her husband.... Many times a husband becomes so preoccupied with his responsibilities in the church that he almost unconsciously neglects the legitimate needs of his wife and family. Even as Jesus gave Himself first to the church, so must the husband first give himself to his wife. A wife needs to know by words, as well as by actions, that she is deeply cherished by her husband....

It is precisely because of the significance of an Elder's role in the church that his marriage is often under the greatest attack....[8]

"Headship" and "Submission"

Hence these paradigms of servanthood, reflected in the biblical mandates of "headship" and "submission" in the Christian marriage relationship, are far from the legalistic interpretations of most evangelical Christian teachings and from the "anything goes" emphasis of modern feminism. The issue is *mutual servanthood*. The "authority" involved in headship and submission exists only to the extent that each spouse is *releasing* Christ indwelling to *minister* to the other.

In summary, "headship" means to provide a *covering* of protection, safety, comfort, and provision. Crabb clearly defines this term:

Headship is a distinctive form of the authority to serve that belongs to the husband, not simply because he is the husband, but because he is a man, because he is masculine. A husband exercises headship over a wife when he expresses his manhood toward her, when he gently but strongly leads her with a strength that is not afraid to become deeply involved and with a maintained sense of direction that expresses strongly held convictions. ... A man longs to feel complete. Whether single or married, he wants to know[9] that he can move toward a woman and touch her deeply [in ways beyond financial provision and sexual pleasures]. ... A woman wants to know[10] that the deepest parts of her being are richly enjoyed by a man who will therefore treat her with tenderness and look at her with delight, someone who will enjoy her because she is enjoyable, not because of a manipulative desire that hopes to get from her what will bring pleasure to him.

...for a man to overcome his doubts...(1) he must focus on God and all that it means to be forgiven, accepted, and called until he is persuaded that there is real strength in acknowledged weakness...(2) He must focus on his wife. ...[and] accept his responsibilities as head of his home and to carry them out in godly fashion....[11]

In short, "submission" means to be in dynamic rapport and harmony with someone. Crabb again offers some powerful insights:

Submission [is]...an opportunity to touch a husband's masculinity with a wife's femininity. ..."a disposition to yield to the husband's authority and an inclination to follow his leadership."

Most men...in moments of painful honesty, would admit to some uncertainty about their own effectiveness in achieving something of real value.... When an other-centered woman discerns the deep questions that plague her husband as he carries on with life...she will sense a desire within herself to respond to that question. ...as she understands her "authority to serve" as the defining purpose in her life, her new heart will respond....[12]

5. What Should We Do With Our Sex Drives in the Meantime?

Until we become *complete* and *mature* in Christ, we still labor to some extent under the Adamic curse, and our natural sex drive remains *a powerful force demanding gratification.* This brings up the issue of "conjugal rights" in marriage relationships. Paul wrote, "The wife does not have authority over her own body, but the husband does; and likewise also the husband does not have authority over his own body, but the wife does" (1 Cor. 7:4). Many have interpreted this to mean that wives and husbands are to yield to each other's sexual needs, and this is correct—but it means much more.

The *context* of First Corinthians 7:4 concerns the *entire person* whose body is "a temple of the Holy Spirit"—not merely sexual relationships (1 Cor. 6:19). The word translated as "body" is *soma*, which refers to the entire person, including the soul and spirit. Both husband and wife are to become one in the Spirit of the indwelling Christ. Sex is merely one of the many emotional instruments God gave us to help us reach that oneness. In all of these, the Spirit of the indwelling Christ alone *enables* us to become one. *As the Holy Spirit of Christ Jesus rules* in each marriage partner, they should continually flow in Christ *toward oneness* with each other in every "instrument" God has given them—specifically including sexual relations.

What should *single* persons do with their sex drives? Sexual *self*-gratification and sexual release are still forms of *self* apart from marriage and Christ's indwelling. Our biblical solution is to "reckon ourselves dead to them" (see Rom. 6:6-11, especially verse 11)! This demands mental discipline and physical *self*-control, which most of us find unpleasant and very painful. It may seem difficult, if not impossible, but it is the only answer that will *work*!

The biblical solution *is* possible—it is possible to control the human sex drive (contrary to the claims of government and education officials)—but *not by our own efforts*! Mere *negative* mental discipline isn't enough to help us avoid being sexually aroused. We must positively discipline our thoughts by "taking our thoughts captive" and focusing them on the indwelling Christ (see 2 Cor. 10:5)!

Still, we are in great danger in this area. Remember, *human sexuality is our greatest area of weakness*. Sexual arousal has both a soulish/spiritual and a physiological element, and they both "demand" satisfaction. For the male, sexual arousal is both *physiological*, involving intrinsic stimulation by the seminal vesicles, and *spiritual/soulical*, involving his need for appreciation and respect for his efforts to give and provide. For the female, sexual arousal is *primarily spiritual/soulical*, centering on her need for security through the unconditional love and acceptance of her companion.

Whether a person is married or single, *sexual arousal demands release*. In all cases, sexual arousal *without release* is an emotionally painful experience. Achieving sexual release within marriage for *self-gratification* (to merely alleviate the pain of sexual arousal) only aggravates the tensions of a marriage. The single person can only seek sexual release *outside of marriage*. This choice comes in only three forms, adultery, homosexuality/lesbianism, and masturbation (both male and female forms). Each of these forms of sexual release are without Christ. When we commit these acts, we are in spiritual darkness and wide open to the influence and bondage of satanic forces that lead us unto destruction. Also note: the flesh can never be satisfied; the more we pamper the flesh, the more it demands of us!

The only solution for us, whether we are married or single, is to *take Christ's indwelling very seriously,* for He is the only way. Paul wrote, "No *temptation* has overtaken you but such as is common to man; and God is faithful, who will not allow you to be *tempted beyond what you are able,* but with the temptation will *provide the way of escape also,* that you may be able to endure it" (1 Cor. 10:13, italics mine). This promise works in practice in only two ways: (a) we must discipline our thoughts onto Christ to see that "way of escape," and (b) the only way to "endure the temptation" is by allowing the indwelling Christ to enable and empower us. There are no shortcuts: *His power is never separated from His Presence.* God's power is deployed in and through us *only as we focus* our minds and attention onto Christ in us, as we deliberately *align our wills* with His.

Whenever we fail in our mental discipline to avoid sexual arousal, we are deeply vulnerable. Both adultery and homosexuality/lesbianism are clearly identified throughout the Scriptures as sin. Masturbation is another matter. Masturbation is by far the most common way by which Christians and non-believers alike seek release from the pain of sexual arousal. Some argue that unlike adultery and homosexuality, masturbation isn't actually forbidden as a sin in the Ten Commandments. Nevertheless, it is dangerous to avoid the issue by hiding behind a legalistic interpretation of

Scripture. Jesus clearly labeled all sexual activity apart from proper marital relations as sin when He extended the definition of adultery to the very thoughts and intents of the heart! (See Matthew 5:28-30.) Even if you rationalize away masturbation as not being a "sin," the fact remains that it leads to very dangerous thinking patterns. (We discuss the destructiveness of masturbation in Chapter 10.)

We must *choose* the mental discipline of focusing on Christ to avoid non-marital sexual arousal in the first place! Yes, it's a difficult choice, but how strongly do we desire to be like Christ?

6. The Full Sixfold Covenant

The truly Christ-centered marriage is nothing less than a *sixfold covenant*. This consists of reciprocal (twofold) covenants between the husband, the wife, and the Lord Christ Jesus. Each spouse lives to be a love-motivated servant of the other. Each also lives to serve Christ. A threefold cord is not easily broken (see Eccles. 4:12), and the sixfold marriage covenant is designed to form the bedrock of society and the Church on earth.

"Self" or the "sin nature" is the greatest hindrance to the sixfold covenant marriage relationship. We constantly try to satisfy our needs by our own efforts and through personal relationships. The fact is that our spouses and family members are human. They are not capable of providing total fulfillment, security, or significance to us—no matter how hard they try or how much they love us. Since only the indwelling Jesus Christ can meet these needs, our loved ones will inevitably disappoint us in time.

When this happens, we build subtle barriers or walls (psychologists call them "defense mechanisms") to "distance" us from the pain our loved ones "cause" through their inability to satisfy. This in turn leads to more distancing, disappointment, and disillusionment on both sides of our relationships.

Dr. Crabb noted:

Both husbands and wives have legitimate personal needs which press for satisfaction. These personal [i.e., psychological] needs are as real as our physical needs. It is impossible to function effectively if these needs are not met....

This state of affairs creates a dilemma. Both my wife and I have real personal needs for love and respect that must be met if we are to treat each other as we should [Ephesians 5:21]. ...I cannot fully love her until I sense that I am a loved, worthwhile person. ...She cannot truly love me until she knows that she is a deeply secure woman. ...I really cannot expect her to treat me properly until she feels loved. Yet I am unable to provide her with the love she needs until someone meets my needs.

Most couples today live behind thick protective walls of emotional distance that block any hope for developing substantial oneness at the level of our deepest personal needs....

The most accepting wife in the world cannot meet her husband's need for significance. ... The most loving husband in the world can never meet his wife's need for security. The stain of self-centeredness has discolored every motivation within us.... *We simply are not enough for each other.*[13]

The only way to stop this otherwise inevitable deterioration of the most vital of our interpersonal relationships is to *embrace the pain*. This involves tearing down our walls or barriers. Then the indwelling Christ can work *through us* to minister His love, acceptance, value, etc. to our spouses—regardless of the personal cost to us.

God calls us to: (a) put aside our *self-seeking* for significance, fulfillment, and self-worth, and to abandon ourselves utterly unto Him; and (b) tear down the inner barriers we erected to shield us from being hurt by others (we are to "die to self" as required in Romans 6:2-14).

Both spouses in a marriage rarely mature in Christ simultaneously. Yet "family oneness" is totally impossible outside of Christ abiding in *both* husband and wife. We must act in faith by trusting God to "straighten out" our spouses, and accept the primary responsibility to yield to His purging within *us* first! We must approach "this dying business" with the attitude, "If anybody is going to start this, it might as well start with me, and *my personal obedience* to Christ within me."

7. Prayer Partnership in Marriage

The most ideal relationship between Christian husbands and wives is a *prayer partnership*. Prayer unites two partners in spirit as no other joint activity can. Only this type of unity in spirit can bring about *total intimacy* in the marriage (body, soul, *and spirit*). A full prayer partnership powerfully augments a marriage because it effectively "covers" each partner during those times when they are "out of touch" spiritually or are too emotionally pressed to stand in faith on a matter. Intercession in prayer partnership is our most direct way to fulfill our basic role as "agents" of the Lord Christ Jesus' love, acceptance, value, and direction to our spouses.

But a full prayer partnership is the most difficult of all human interpersonal relationships to achieve in marriage. Because prayer partnership requires a total openness and honesty, it is easier for two people of the same gender to achieve full prayer partnership than it is for a husband and wife. This mutual and unconditional acceptance of one another is perhaps the rarest—and yet the most vital—attribute of a healthy marriage. It requires a level of love, inner security, and mutual trust that is far beyond most Christian marriages.

Most partners strongly desire closeness and intimacy before marriage and in the early phase of married relationship. But at best they only reach the "comfort level," for they fear that their spouses will reject them if they get to know "the real" person hidden within. Most marriage partners unknowingly erect personal barriers against intimacy that no one is allowed to penetrate, particularly someone as "threatening" as a spouse. Full prayer partnership draws both partners across those hidden barriers, causing buried fears to arise with new barriers and distancing. Few if any marriages ever get over these inward fears.

End Notes: Chapter Three

1. Grubb, Norman. *Once Caught, No Escape—My Life Story* (Fort Washington, PA: Christian Literature Crusade, 1969), Second Impression 1971, p. 205.

2. Crabb, Lawrence J., Jr. *Men & Women* (Grand Rapids, MI: Zondervan Publishing House, 1991), pp. 155-156. Copyright ©1991 by Lawrence J. Crabb, Jr. Used by permission of Zondervan Publishing House.

3. Rekers, George Alan. "Psychological Foundations from Rearing Masculine Boys and Feminine Girls," *Recovering Biblical Manhood and Womanhood: A Response to Evangelical Feminism*, eds. John Piper and Wayne Gruden (Wheaton, IL: Good New Publishers, 1991), Ch. 17, pp. 305-306. Used by permission of Good News Publishers, Crossway Books, Wheaton, Illinois 60187.

4. Crabb, Lawrence J., Jr. *Inside Out* (Colorado Springs, CO: NavPress, 8th printing, 1989), pp. 208-209. Copyright © 1989 by Lawrence J. Crabb, Jr. Used by permission of NavPress. All rights reserved. For copies, call 1-800-366-7788.

5. God calls us to become "complete" in three ways: (a) *individually* in communion with God; (b) as *husband-wife units* to fulfill our God-ordained roles in "multiplying" mature Christians on earth; and (c) *collectively* to

physically manifest the presence and ministry of Christ on earth as the Body of Christ.

6. Schmitt, Dorothy. "Being An Elder's Wife." Pamphlet published by Fellowship of Believers, 210 Third Ave. NE, Grand Rapids, MN 55744.

7. This word is not found in the New Testament but is used extensively in non-biblical ancient Greek writings.

8. Schmitt. "Being An Elder's Wife."

9. Unless, of course, his masculinity has been seriously distorted by dysfunctionally-rooted self-protecting strategies.

10. Unless, of course, her femininity has been seriously distorted by dysfunctionally-rooted self-protecting strategies.

11. Crabb. *Men & Women*, pp. 198-201. Copyright © 1991 by Lawrence J. Crabb, Jr. Used by permission of Zondervan Publishing House.

12. Crabb. *Men & Women*, pp. 202-208. Copyright © 1991 by Lawrence J. Crabb, Jr. Used by permission of Zondervan Publishing House.

13. Crabb, Lawrence J., Jr. *The Marriage Builder* (Grand Rapids, MI: Zondervan Publishing House, 1982), pp. 26,33-34. Copyright © 1982 by The Zonderan Corporation. Used by permission of Zondervan Publishing House.

Chapter Four

Essentials of Love-Motivated Servanthood

I have personally made the marvelous observation that there is nothing more deeply satisfying than discovering Christ Jesus has used me to benefit someone else. This satisfaction is particularly strong when that "someone" is my spouse or some other "loved one"!

Agape love is a major aspect of the release of the "eternal life" of Jesus Christ to others. This can only occur as the indwelling Holy Spirit of Christ Jesus releases His light, life, and love through us. But that occurs only to the same extent that we yield to Him. In order to be a vessel of Christ's love, we must set aside all the distancing barriers erected with our self-protecting goals, strategies, and behavior.

On the other hand, the very service of extending *agape* love can be painful if we are unprepared in Christ. When we extend love to those who need it the most, they often respond with rejection or opposition. We must not allow those hurts hurled against us to intimidate or otherwise hinder us from conveying Christ's love to them.

or word, power + love

This is especially important when we are extending this love to our spouses. The inescapable fact is that our hurts—whether they are old hurts from the past, or new hurts inflicted by a spouse who rejects our *agape* love—appear to be "life threatening". That is because we are looking to another person, no matter how "special" he or she is to us, as our source of acceptance, purpose, and fulfillment. The only way out of the vicious circle of hurt and dysfunctional reactions is to turn to the indwelling Christ Jesus as the Source.

1. Christ's Love, Presence, and Authority Are Inseparable

Again, *love-motivated servanthood* is absolutely essential for a fully Christ-centered marriage relationship, and for *all* interpersonal relationships in the Body of Christ. Any interpersonal relationship not rooted in Spirit-empowered and love-motivated servanthood is neither Christ-honoring nor Christ-serving!

Love-motivated servanthood carries with it the very authority of Christ. But this authority is *never* separated from His presence. It will only be manifested through us when we are fully committed and yielded to Him. Only then will His light, life, and love flow into and through us as He wills.

Just as the authority of Christ is never separated from His presence, so are love and commitment inseparable. The bottom line is that there must be *commitment* to love-motivated servanthood *before there will be a manifestation* of love-motivated servanthood as empowered by the Holy Spirit of the indwelling Christ!

Meekness is related to this. *Meekness* is a greatly misunderstood word. The Greek word translated as "meekness" is *proates*, which means "having great power and authority, and knowing it, but being gentle and patient in its exercise." *Only kings can truly do this.*

Why is biblical meekness so rare? Why are rebellion and suppression so often the norm in our marriages, families, and churches? The answer is: *insecurity!* To be meek, we must *have authority* and *be secure* in our knowledge of having it. Each of us must personally yield all to Christ and individually be certain of our security in Him. It requires us to have the "Philippians 2:3-8 attitude" of *agape* love, where we view each other as of *equal value and standing* in Christ. In this environment, each believer is of great value, and is neither a threat to a leader's personal security nor someone to be manipulated by the leader.

Equality in *value* and *standing* does not imply equality or duplication of *function* or *roles* in Christ. We are *equal but different.* We complement one another in function and role in marriage, in the Body of Christ, and in church leadership. Each of us has been *called* and *qualified* by God to do specific things that others are not called to do in the same way and place. The Body of Christ is very diverse, and it is comprised of innumerable and unique individuals, each carefully set into a special place in Christ's Body.

As we are responsible for others to serve or minister in whatever areas be ours, then we have the full authority of Christ to meet that responsibility. We edify the Body of Christ when we function properly in our places. This happens when each of us: (a) learns (experientially, not just mentally) to *function* in our individual calling or ministry; and (b) becomes *responsible* in our functioning in context with other believers. Authority, responsibility, and the presence of Christ indwelling are inseparable, and so are love, commitment and subordination.

2. Keys to Love-Motivated Servanthood

Four key elements are required in the stable Christian marriage relationship (and in virtually every calling of God). All of them are forms of love-motivated servanthood. These elements are (a) walking in faith believing, (b) intercession, (c) encouragement, and (d) discernment.

Walking in Faith Believing—The First Key to Love-Motivated Servanthood

...if you have faith...even if you say to this mountain, "Be taken up and cast into the sea," it shall happen (Matthew 21:21).

Truly, truly, I say to you, he who believes in Me, the works that I do shall he do also; and greater... (John 14:12).

When we compare our present experiences with these statements and other passages of Scripture, it becomes clear just how much we lack true *spiritual potency*. Most of us try to "pray in faith believing." Most Christians think that "believing" means something like praying or acting "as if a particular statement or promise or claim is true, *never allowing oneself to think that it might not be.*" Then, if we see no results, we say, "We failed because we didn't have enough faith; we had doubt and unbelief," or "His answer was no," or even worse, "Well, those promises are not for us today." *What kind of faith is that?*

Faith is not a "thing" *per se,* but a dynamic aspect of our personal relationship with our Lord Christ! Acting "in faith believing" has four aspects: (a) seeing Him in His spiritual reality; (b) aligning our will with His; (c) dynamically depending upon Him as that spiritual Person; and (d) sensitively obeying Him with a motive of love.

Biblical prayer and ministry "in faith believing" *begins* with discovering *God's will* and aligning our will with His—not the reverse. Most of us decide what we want and try to badger, beg, or bribe God into alignment with our wills. That is not faith; it is presumption. Faith is not mental determination; it is an inner working of the Holy Spirit giving us a total assurance that we are acting in line with God's purposes and will.

Norman Grubb described how this principle was learned in the early days of the Worldwide Evangelization Crusade:

> We had, however, begun to observe another emphasis in the prayer lives of the men of the Bible. We saw that they went much further back than we did. *They first discovered whether their prayer was God's will; then having received assurance on this point,* they prayed, received by faith, persisted, declared things to come, with all the authority of God Himself.[1]

Martyn Lloyd-Jones, in his book *Joy Unspeakable,* argues powerfully from the Scriptures that this depth of guidance and assurance is available to believers today. After describing two levels or types of assurance most Christians obtain by logical scriptural arguments, he says this:

> But there is a third type of assurance, which is the highest, the most absolute and glorious, and which differs essentially from the other two. ... the glory of this third and highest form of assurance is that it is neither anything that we do, nor any deduction that we draw, but an assurance that is given to us by the blessed Spirit himself.

Now if you like, it is again the whole difference between Romans 8:15 and Romans 8:16. ... Our [human] spirit has been crying "Abba, Father," but over and above that the [Holy] Spirit now bears witness with our [human] spirit—He confirms ours saying to us: "You are right." The Spirit does it. Now this is neither our action, nor our deduction, but the immediate witness of the Spirit, and that is why it is both so absolute and so certain.[2]

Several Bible passages reveal God's will for our marriage relationships. We *know with assurance* that it is God's will for our marriages to be truly a sixfold covenant in Christ! We *know with assurance* that it is God's will that our Lord Christ Jesus truly be our source, or Tree of Life! We *know with assurance* that it is God's will that husbands and wives be true full prayer partners.

Intercession—The Second Key to Love-Motivated Servanthood

The ministry of intercession is *vital* in both the Christian marriage relationship and Christian fellowships, to undergird love-motivated and Spirit-empowered discernment and servanthood. However, that intercession must also be done in unity of vision.

There is a significant difference between *prayer* and *intercession*. The essence of that difference is the extent to which *we* are thusly walking in faith believing and functioning in the *dynamics* of the *spiritual* plane.

Intercession is our soul entering into His *spiritual presence*. We also enter into His presence *cognitively* (with our mind). Then, as His *agent*, we exercise His authority and creative power. Intercession, therefore, is primarily a *spiritual* exercise, even though it requires much mental discipline on our part.

We bring our entire person into His presence when we intercede in prayer. We take all needs, requests, and petitions *onto ourself* personally, *identifying* with them and *becoming* them. When we come into intercession on behalf of another, we come *as* that person. We *identify* personally with him or her.

First, we must determine the Lord's will in each matter of concern. Once we *know with assurance* His will in a matter, we do not simply *ask or request* Him to do it; we *declare* that it be so in the authority of His Name and by the power of His shed blood. That declaration involves our will or choice for it; it is an *inward* determination in the *assurance* that we have simply declared God's will on the matter and that the spiritual power of our Lord Christ Jesus will effect it.

Giving Encouragement—The Third Key to Love-Motivated Servanthood

Encouragement is at the heart of all forms of love-motivated servanthood, particularly in the loving service of the *comforter*, the giver of *mercy*, the *helper*, and the *exhorter* (see Rom. 12:8; 1 Cor. 12:28). Lawrence Crabb and Dan Allender tell us;

> ...in all that is done, we must keep two pivotal truths clearly in mind:
>
> 1. People are hurting more deeply than we know (and more than they themselves sometimes know, like the person who is not yet aware that cancer has formed in his body);
>
> 2. Relationship with Christ provides resources unique and indispensable to substantially heal ...now and...perfectly heal...forever.[3]

Only the supernatural empowerment of the Holy Spirit can equip us to genuinely love, accept, and value others with purity of heart. *Servanthood* demands that we minister with pure motives, not to obtain fulfillment for ourselves through giving. We minister solely to edify others in Christ. *Empowerment* demands that we always allow *Christ in us,* not merely to provide us with guidance, but also to *enable* us to pay the personal costs of time and emotional stress inevitable in ministry. We must be committed to people, not to a *"ministry."*

Discerning Needs and Counseling—The Fourth Key to Love-Motivated Servanthood

The starting point when ministering encouragement to others is to understand their hurts and needs. After first seeking that understanding directly from the Lord, we need to talk with those who need encouragement to fill in the details. Our very interaction with them is often an important part of the ministry itself! We should always communicate our *desire to understand and empathize,* and clearly let them know that we (still) *recognize their worth.* Then we should help them recognize the specific barriers they must submit to the Lord for healing. This requires time to carefully listen and demonstrate that we are actually hearing them.

When we seek to extend *agape* love in servanthood to others, we often find that our own needs get in the way. Although we mean well, we fail to expose ourselves sufficiently to convey the needed love, unconditional acceptance, and value to the person.

Because we come to Christ as imperfect creatures dwelling in a hostile environment, *all* of us need inner heart healing. Each of us must *recognize* our need to take the initiative to become healed and free. Then we must *function* in Christian love to help others in the Body of Christ in *their* inner heart healings. A *breaking* may be required to bring us to the humiliating realization that each of us needs inner heart healing. That makes it possible for us to be *plunged* into Christ's lordship over *total* self. Finally, we then are able to be used by our Lord in counseling other believers in their inner healings.

3. The Need for Total Honesty and Openness

Each marriage (and every divine "calling") is a form of love-motivated servanthood. It requires *honesty and effective unity with the other member(s) of the Body of Christ.*

As we emphasized in the preceding chapter, in the true sixfold covenant marriage relationship, both partners should first and foremost be prayer partners! The difficulty is that prayer partnership requires that each partner know many of the intimate details about the other partner's weaknesses and strengths. Furthermore, they must fully accept each other, and seek to edify their mate anyway! *That requires total honesty and openness with each other.* It is only through honesty and openness that the two can truly be in unity, and trust one another.

Total honesty and openness is essential for trust, and trust is essential for unity. Despite all that has been taught and emphasized about unity among Christians, we are still far from attaining it. Unity eludes our churches and Christian fellowships; it is rare among individual believers within most fellowships! Yet, *effective unity is vital for spiritual potency.* Jesus said, "By this all men will know that you are My disciples, if you have love for one another" (Jn. 13:35).

The main reason we lack true rapport in our marriage relationships (and other relationships within the Body of

Christ) may be that we each are not certain of our security in our personal relationships with Christ Jesus. We do not see ourselves as *equal in value* to our brothers and sisters in Christ; we fear that others will not consider us to be of the same value as they are in Christ. Rebellion reflects our feelings of insecurity, and our fears result only in exhausting works of activity.

Norman Grubb draws on his experiences with the Worldwide Evangelization Crusade to provide some invaluable insights on unity that are applicable here:

> Now let us...apply to the other members of the Body what we have applied to ourselves. Recognize Christ in them: count on Christ in them. In so far as there is another nature observable in them, show them the same tolerance and sympathy as we do to ourselves. Believe that Christ is working Romans 6:11 out in them also.... By so doing we are effecting more than the maintenance of unity; by our faith we are building up our brethren in Christ ... faith is creative....[4]

When we show love, forbearance, acceptance, and encouragement to our brothers and sisters in both attitude and acts—even in the midst of contentions—we actually release Christ in them. How powerfully this admonition applies to the marriage relationship!

End Notes: Chapter Four

1. Grubb, Norman. *Touching The Invisible* (London: Lowe & Brydone Ltd., 1940; 1972 impression [available through Christian Literature Crusade, Fort Washington, PA 19034]), pp. 9-10.

2. Lloyd-Jones, Mertyn. *Joy Unspeakable* (1984), pp. 92-93. Published by special permission with Kingsway Publication, Ltd., Sussex, England. Used by permission of Harold Shaw Publishers, Wheaton, IL.

3. Crabb, Lawrence J., Jr. and Allender, Dan. *Encouragement* (Grand Rapids, MI: Zondervan Publishing House, 1984), p. 15. Copyright © 1984 by The Zondervan Corporation. Used by permission of Zondervan Publishing House.

4. Grubb, Norman. *Touching The Invisible*, p. 45.

Part II

Inner Heart Healing
Unto Servanthood

We began this volume with a detailed understanding of human nature as God reveals it to us in His Holy Scriptures. More specifically, we needed to know: (a) what it means to be "in the image of God"; (b) the depth of the original sin in us; (c) how Christ, living within the heart of believers, heals and restores us to the extent we choose to allow Him to; and (d) the nature of our inner heart struggles to experientially appropriate that healing and restoration.

We now study in detail those inner heart struggles and the process of their healings—especially in our marriage relationships—so we may be all our Lord Christ Jesus wills for us. Deep repentance, leading to full trust and dependence upon and obedience to Christ living in us, is necessary for healing our inner hearts, and restoring vibrancy to Christian living. Even in most "Spirit-filled" Christian marriages today, we are far from that.

This section looks at how the Holy Spirit of the indwelling Christ leads and empowers each of us through the deep repentance that happens as we yield to Him, and to release the indwelling Holy Spirit to work through us.

Chapter Five

What Is Inner
Heart Healing?

One day in mid-December of 1988, as I was meditating on the Lord, He brought to my mind many of the individuals in the Pentacostal fellowship I attended at the time, including those in leadership. I was shocked to realize by the Spirit that every one of these "mature" Christians had deep, heartbreaking inner heart problems, especially in their marriage relationships! They had kept these problems well-hidden from others, but they had been struggling with them for years without victory, and now they lacked the "joy of their salvation" and vibrancy in their witness of Christ. Worst of all, despite a genuine commitment to serving Christ, they were close to "burn-out" and despair.

Our Lord only shows us the weaknesses of others so we will minister to them, whether in prayer and intercession or also in personal encouragement and practical help. We are never to destroy the dignity and self-worth of another through our words or actions. This is one of the most important reasons that such knowledge is to be kept in total confidentiality.

This particular revelation was also disturbing to me for other reasons. First, I was shocked at how *widespread* this need for inner heart healing is among "Spirit-filled" Christians. I knew that I had similar personal needs but I thought that at least my fellow Christians had "their act together" (it appeared that way).

Second, and even more devastating to me, was the realization that *I did not have the answers for them, and I was in exactly the same situation as they*! I felt I had been God's Bible teacher of "power for the hour," yet my "knowledge" of the Scriptures wasn't helping me, let alone others. What an ego-buster!

Robert S. McGee lists four lies of satan prevalent in modern society that defeat even "Spirit-filled, Bible-believing" Christians in their personal lives. Two of the four lies are of particular interest here: (a) "My personal value and self-worth depends upon what I do, accomplish or produce"; and (b) "My personal value and self-worth depends upon my being accepted and respected by other people."[1]

Most of us know *intellectually* that our personal value and self-worth come only from Christ Jesus and not from anything we can do. After all, that is a basic tenet of biblical Christian faith. Why, then, are we still bound to such thinking and its destructive ramifications?

Galatians 2:20 and other Scripture passages clearly state the incredible truth that Christ Himself *lives within us* as His Holy Spirit. Since He makes available to us all the power and ability we will ever need to be set free, why aren't we living in freedom?

The first step toward understanding this dilemma is to understand what the Bible actually says about our inner human nature—our "psychological" makeup. We have a human spirit as well as soul. Christians have two forms of life, or live in two realms. We function in both the spiritual and physical domains, and we function according to either of two purposes or goals: self-will or Christ's will. "Eternal life" is the very presence and life of Christ in us! He lives in us to *empower us to live righteously according to love-motivated servanthood*. We are to trust and hope in Him to meet our needs, and not seek to have them met by our own efforts!

Original sin runs so deep in us that even after years of "walking in the Spirit," we are still largely self-seekers rather than Christ-bearers. This is but a hint of the depth to which we must repent!

Ahah! Light at last! Since true repentance at that depth is a difficult step for us to make, most of us don't even try. Just considering it increases our inner sense of guilt. It's extremely difficult because we don't know how to repent at that level; and when we find out how, we know it will be excruciatingly painful. We remain oblivious to the fact that this inner pain was created by God to drive us to total dependence upon and obedience to Christ indwelling. So we just continue to hide our inner hurts through various cover ups, pretending to be holy Christians by our actions. We cope with these inner hurts through various "defense mechanism" maintained to distance ourselves from others whom we sense might hurt us further.

Victory over our inner hurts, hang-ups, and secret sins only comes as we truly repent from self-seeking and from seeking our "identity and fulfillment" from the "tree of knowledge"—outside of God's direct provision. True faith is total dependence upon and obedience to the indwelling Spirit of Christ, our Tree of Life. Our Lord is revealing to those of us who are truly willing to face this difficult and painful task just what it involves, and how to begin. We can only begin to make appropriate choices as we begin to grasp the fullness and inner assurance of Christ in our human spirits.

1. The Holy Spirit Empowers Healing Repentance

Victory comes as a process over time, as we learn to totally depend upon and obey the indwelling Christ in all things. It requires a discipline of deep repentance that is impossible to achieve without a complete focus on Christ, with an absolute assurance that He indeed dwells within. Even our faith ultimately comes from God.

Reckoned to Be Dead to Self-Seeking

We escape the monster of the "self-life" only *by dying* to it—by choosing to act separately from it. Sadly, most of us also have to overcome a lifetime of "religious conditioning" through the painful way of brokenness at the hand of the Lord. Rick Joyner noted:

> Anyone may teach about God's love, but only those who have laid down their lives with Him can impart that love. Anyone can teach truths, but only those who have given their lives in search of it can impart a love for the truth, which is the essence of the true teaching ministry. The knowledge and ability to impart facts can easily be attained through study and practice; the apostolic ability to impart life can only be attained by taking up our crosses daily, following Him, and like Him, doing all things for the sake of the gospel.[2]

The Epistle to the Romans makes it clear that we are to reckon ourselves dead to sin and self! (See Romans 6:6,11.) Verses 6 and 11 contain two strong words of action that we are to do: *knowing* and *consider/reckon*. Both words speak of mental discipline on our part! They require us to deliberately choose to think a certain way, whether we feel like it or not, whether we "believe" that it makes sense or not.

Self-Protecting Goals, Strategies, and Behavior

God created mankind with unique needs that draw us to Him. These include (a) the need to be valued as a servant; (b) the need to have a sense of significance, and purpose; and (c) the need to have others receive our servanthood. We recombine these basic needs into two categories: the need for *fulfillment* and the need for *acceptance*, along with their respective opposites, *emptiness* and *rejection*. These deep needs are rooted in the human *spirit*, and can only be met by the life of the *indwelling* Christ.

These needs, being in our human spirit, have very strong influences on us. To the extent that we are in Christ, He meets these needs, and we are truly in peace. But to the extent that we are under the Adamic curse, we try (inevitably in vain) to find the fulfillment of these needs by our own self-seeking efforts to manipulate others. The inevitable disappointments appear to be intense life-threatening hurts.

These needs of our human spirits are among the most powerful long-term motivating forces in our lives. They also play a major role in hindering us from being all our Lord Christ Jesus wills for us. Transferring our seeking of their fulfillment from *self*-effort to yielding to Christ as our Tree of Life, is the essence of inner heart healing. To live by the fruit of the Tree of Life (Christ indwelling) is to ever live in love-motivated and Spirit-empowered servanthood—to minister to the needs of others, not to those of ourself.

Dr. Myles Munroe noted in his book, *In Pursuit of Purpose:*

> The greatest tragedy in life is not death, but life without reason. ... The deepest craving of the human spirit is to find a sense of significance and relevance. The search for relevance in life is the ultimate pursuit of man.[3]

When we live for *self* (i.e., by the "tree of knowledge"), those needs go unmet, and that lack strongly influences our livelong goals, strategies, and behavior. These unmet needs powerfully dominate our marriages and other interpersonal relationships, usually in ways of which we are unaware. Furthermore, out of self-protection, we form intrinsic distancing barriers between ourselves and those closest to us. We need specific forms of deep repentance in order to experience inner healing of these things.

This search for purpose deeply affects our marriage relationships. David Wilkerson in his book, *Have You Felt Like Giving Up Lately?* noted:

> When your relationship with the Lord is wrong, it affects all human relationships. Most Christian married couples are not having trouble with their marriages. Rather, they are having trouble with God, with faith, with prayer; therefore, they have trouble with each other.[4]

When spouses, friends, and acquaintances fail to meet our needs of the spirit (which they are unable to satisfy), we respond by putting up barriers, or by "distancing" ourselves from them. This process of holding unrealistic expectations, experiencing hurt when our needs aren't met, followed by rejection and distancing, ultimately causes marriages to fail.

Only Christ, as our Tree (source) of Life, can provide those needs at the deepest level of satisfaction. Yet we constantly and intensely strive, in unconscious ways, to meet those needs through our relationships with other persons, especially our spouses. Their inevitable failure to meet our needs (God never equipped them to) acerbates our striving efforts.

The salvation process must be allowed to complete its course in our lives and marriage relationships. Any other course leads to unbearable pain and frustration. Apart from the life and power of the *indwelling Christ,* the human spirit is but a hollow inner core, a deep void churning with deep needs unmet. Most of us approach life unaware of the distinction between our soulical and spiritual needs. As a result, we make demands on our loved ones that they can never meet—even if they are willing to try. We all need human companionship, and God designed marriage and friendship to effectively meet this "soulical" need. But we all also have the *spiritual* need for fulfillment, for security in love and significance in self-worth, and we must learn that these can be met only by Christ dwelling within us, never by our spouses, family members, or acquaintances.

The emptiness of the human spirit is the deepest level at which we make the *foundational* choices of our lives: *goals* we will seek in order to avoid, minimize, or at least cope with the pain of that emptiness. We usually make these basic choices in response to earlier traumatic times of pain. The specific goals we then choose often depend upon the particular traumatic circumstances. Nevertheless, we do establish goals. Inevitably, once they are chosen, they *drive* us throughout our lives. But we usually soon forget both (a) that we *did* establish these goals by our free choice and so are always capable of "unchoosing" them; and (b) *why* we chose those goals.

The next deepest level at which we make choices that dominate our lives, is where we adopt *strategies* to meet these personal goals. It is at this *strategy* level that the demonic-reinforced dark thinking patterns are buried, that the emotional empowerments become embedded. Once these strategies are chosen, they *drive* our *behavior*. Again, we usually soon forget both (a) that we *did* establish these strategies by our free choice, and so are always capable of "unchoosing" them; and (b) *why* we chose those strategies.

Many people use such distancing strategies. Perfectionism, dominance over others, workaholism, etc., are common examples in both the secular world and Christian ministry.

The top level at which we make choices is the one where our *acts or behavior* patterns follow those strategies. But, again, we seldom recognize them as the *free choices* they are. Since our self-protecting choices of goals and strategies are so deeply hidden from our consciousness by then, we do not realize that they can be reversed by counter-choices. Rather, we feel *driven* or *forced* "by the way life is" to act the way we do. That is the trap we live in.

The "What" And "How" of Required Repentance

For the Christian marriage and other interpersonal relationships in the Body of Christ, dying to self *via* surrender-repentance is particularly important in regards to these self-protecting and self-seeking goals, strategies, and behaviors, especially when they are rooted in early traumatic experiences.

The choice to simply "repent" from inappropriate or destructive behavior will not produce victory over dysfunctionally-rooted traumas and our protective reactions to them. We must have to understand how we instinctively avoid the pain of emptiness and worthlessness deep within. This involves learning the particular forms of pain we strive to avoid, and the strategies we formed to avoid them. This is especially important because those strategies are the forces behind our inappropriate and destructive behavior.

All of our choices to avoid pain result from failure to truly trust Christ within as being sufficient to meet our needs. Final victory requires a painful confrontation with those deep-seated pains, followed by a difficult struggle to replace our sense of emptiness and worthlessness with genuine and profound faith in the indwelling Christ.

Repentance is *something we do*; it is one of the few things that Christ in us does *not* do. Repentance requires an act of will that invokes the *discipline needed for change.* We cannot choose that discipline without knowing the precise, specific, and detailed aspects of the dark thought patterns that need to be changed.

How do we repent? We must totally surrender every area of darkness to Christ. This "surrender" requires *total involvement*, not mere mental or emotional exercise. It is an act of our will, as we seek Christ with our entire being, with every resource, thought, and feeling at our disposal. The "breaking" process is a choice we make out of desperation as an act of faith:

1. We repent unto Christ indwelling; then He in us empowers it! As we *choose* to change Christ gives us the *power* to change.

2. We pray with intensity. Prayer releases Christ. Praying in faith believing is first ascertaining God's will[5] in the situation, then responding accordingly.

3. We offer our prayers with praise and worship. By focusing our attention on God, we clear our channel of communication with Him.

4. We reject and hate all sin in our lives. This is not just the acts of sin we have committed; it refers to our very sin-nature itself.

5. We *reckon* our self to be crucified with Christ (see Rom. 6:6,11). This requires committed determination (see 2 Cor. 10:5).

6. We renounce self and refuse to live *on our own* in the old way (see 1 Cor. 10:13).

7. We put aside all our own efforts to seek significance, fulfillment, and self-worth, abandoning ourselves utterly unto Him.

8. We tear down the inner barriers we have erected to keep from being hurt by others.

9. We act in all things as if these reckonings are *fact*, regardless of feelings or even mental "disbelief."

10. We embrace the indwelling Christ. We desire, welcome, want, seek, and heartily consent to Him living His life in and through us, when and as He chooses.

11. We fast as needed to help us hear God more clearly, putting aside all things that hinder or distract us from deep union with Christ. As we put aside the desires of the flesh, the Spirit works more powerfully and effectively in us; grace flows more

easily; we see the innermost root causes of problems more clearly; and we sense Christ's love for us more vividly.

Although the process of repentance in our individual inner heart healing may not involve *all* 11 disciplines, it always involves establishing who is the actual source of our sense of personal worth, purpose, identity, acceptance, and fulfillment. This source is either our Lord Christ Jesus, or other people (i.e., our spouse). It is only when the "Tree of Life" is our source that the hurts we receive from others cease to be life-threatening, and we become free to love others in spite of the hurts they hurl at us.

This form of repentance is "surrender," and it is based upon a deep understanding of Christ's atoning work on Calvary. We have been carefully [and correctly] taught that Christ died on the cross to pay the penalty or "wages" for our sins, which is death (see Rom. 6:23). When we accept that atonement, we have the assurance of "living forever" (i.e., in Heaven). In that context, "repentance" means (a) our (mental) realization of our need for forgiveness; (b) entreating Christ for that forgiveness; and (c) accepting salvation on faith ("faith" here meaning a determined mental discipline of thinking and acting as if it indeed has been done). That is all correct doctrine, *as far as it goes.*

However, Christ died to do *more* than merely remove the penalty and wages of our sins (death); *He intends to remove our very sin-nature!* He died on the cross to remove the presence of sin in our lives "…He has been manifested to put away sin by the sacrifice of Himself" (Heb. 9:26). I believe this is one of the meanings of Isaiah 53:5 "…by His scourging [stripes] we are healed." Our intrinsic *sin nature* is the root cause of all of our sicknesses (both soulish and physical).

God requires commitment to the path of the cross because He knows we are likely to give up when the pain gets stronger in the process of inner heart healing. He has made total healing available to us through Christ Jesus. Our inner wounds literally drive the sins that so easily beset us, so He has commanded us to be free of them through the cross. In Hebrews 12:1, we are told to " lay aside every encumbrance, and the sin which so easily entangles us...." Elsewhere, the Scriptures admonish us to be perfect (*teleios*), which means "to be mature, to reach the end result of our sanctification process" (see Matthew 5:48; 2 Cor. 7:1).

Repentance is not an intellectual step; it is an act rooted in choice/will. We are to consciously and deliberately choose to transfer our weaknesses, illnesses, sins, and self-seeking, self-protecting goals and strategies onto Him on the cross. This process of "transferring" involves four minimum elements:

1. Knowing the "specific" aspects of our sin-nature we are transferring onto Christ on Calvary.

2. "Seeing" Christ on the cross as the receiver of those aspects of our sin-nature.

3. Trusting and yielding to the miraculous inner workings of the indwelling Holy Spirit of Christ Jesus to actually effect that transfer.

4. "Reckoning" it as actually having been accomplished by Him, according to Romans 6!

The first step to inner heart healing is ascertaining exactly what we need to surrender to Christ Jesus at the moment. We must deeply repent in three specific areas to receive inner heart healing and become whole in the Christlike walk.

1. *Our intrinsic aversion to God.* Since we know our personal inadequacies and sinful attitudes, we have a natural tendency to "hide" from God rather than aggressively seek Him and His help as the Lord of our lives!

2. *Our doubts that Christ is really willing and sufficient* to receive and remove these areas of sin or inadequacy, or to protect us from being wounded beyond our ability to recover. We need to understand that His Spirit in us is dealing with our sinfulness in sanctification, not judgment.

3. Our specific self-protecting goals and strategies and habits, and the emotions that accompany and empower them, must be relinquished and confessed.

2. Choosing to Live by Abandonment Unto Christ Indwelling

Several years ago, I received this prophetic message after reading and meditating on Isaiah 30:15:

Why are you so trying to live your lives as Christians by your strength?

Either I am really real in your life, or I am not. If you believe that I am really real in your life, then why are you trying to live your life according to My Word by your own strength?

I have created you with a deep inner void that only My Presence can fill. There is nothing whatsoever that you can do to fill the emptiness in your life; only I can fill it.

This is true repentance, that you stop trying to fill your emptiness by your own efforts, and let Me fill it in you. This is true rest, that you yield to Me indwelling you, that I be released within and through you.

Wholeness can only come as we utterly trust in the faithfulness of the indwelling Christ to meet our needs of security and significance, and cooperate with Him to demonstrate His faithfulness to our loved ones through practical acts of compassion and respect.

Why do we avoid deep repentance and inner healing, even when we realize that the benefits are so incredible? We choose compromise because of shame and unbelief. We need to realize that *everyone* has hidden "inner filthiness," and that its source is usually beyond our control and choice. There is nothing "shameful" about admitting this. None of us "asked" for our sin-nature. But it is shameful for any of us to cling to it in face of so great a salvation and deliverance in Christ!

The Lord will reveal to our conscious minds the things that need to be submitted to His cleansing blood. Each of us—seasoned Bible-believing and Spirit-filled Christians included—must be honest with ourselves! We must acknowledge our areas of failure and need, and believe that healing is possible and available.

The deep repentance needed for inner heart healing is impossible unless we: (a) are broken in each area of self-seeking and dependence upon ourselves; and (b) totally rely on the Lord Christ Jesus for all things. This is hard for us because most of us regard "eternal life" as an abstract concept rather than an *indwelling Person*. Because Christ Jesus lives within us, there are virtually no limits to the victories we can receive simply by our yielding to His lordship. Yet we choose to live only on the "natural" plane, oblivious of His life dwelling within us.

To remain still is not an option for us; passivity in this issue leads to falling back. We face a choice: We can complete the painful inner healing process and make the actual lordship of Christ a reality; or we can choose to compromise, living with unremoved, partially hidden filthiness in our spirits until we "make it to Heaven." In the meantime, most of us will probably slip in our faith and our Christian walk, inadvertently hurting our loved ones.

Crucified With Christ

How do we ever escape? We mentioned earlier that Romans 6:6 and 6:11 make it clear that we are to "reckon ourselves dead to sin" and self!

L.E. Maxwell summarizes this process with some very effective admonitions:

Christ's requirements are indeed unattainables—that you must learn first of all....

Self can never cast out self.... [Quoting James H. McConkey] God lays His foundations deep. Victory over sin He lays in the *depths of death*.

[Concerning Romans 6:11] Note that Paul does not say, reckon sin dead to you. God's way of victory over sin is not through the *suppression* of sinful desires, nor through the *eradication* of the Old Nature, nor yet through the *cleansing* of inbred sin. God's way of victory is through *crucifixion*— deliverance is only through *death*. There is a vast difference between reckoning myself dead to sin and reckoning sin dead to me. Every attempt to make sin dead to me, through self-effort, or struggle, or blessing, or make believe, is not following the scriptural pattern [but rather is by the fruit of the Tree of Knowledge of Good and Evil]. God says

I am to reckon myself dead to sin. If I am willing to be rid of sin, let faith fasten on the fact of my death to sin through my actual life-union with Christ. I am "in Christ." And to be in Him is to be "dead to sin"...[6]

The next-to-last sentence is significant: "...through my actual *life-union* with Christ." The issue is our *identification with Christ*, and our focus is on *Him in us*. This is the watershed issue for Christians for the next decade and beyond; only those who choose to take the indwelling presence of Christ very seriously will be able to overcome!

Christians often become "clogged vessels" of His light, life, and love because of two closely linked barriers: (a) a lack of self-esteem and dignity; and (b) the above discussed self-protecting goals and strategies. Proper self-esteem or self-love isn't self-love in the sense of the sin of pride or false humility; it is a realistic appraisal of *who we actually are in Christ*! Christ considered us of such great value, personal worth, and dignity that He was willing to pay that awesome price on Calvary for our salvation. He wants us to see ourselves the same way. This is the first step in removing everything that hinders and impedes the flow of love from the Lord through us.

The Lord *values* us as a fine craftsman values His work. In His parables of the lost coin and the lost sheep, it was the *value* of the coin/sheep that caused the owner to search to the end.

If we cannot receive His love ourselves, He cannot flow His love through us unto others. This is why the apostle Paul prayed:

That He [God] *would grant you...to be strengthened with power through His Spirit in the inner man; so*

*that Christ may dwell in your hearts through faith;
and that you, being rooted and grounded in love,
may be able to comprehend...and to know the love of
Christ...[and] be filled up to all the fulness of God*
(Ephesians 3:16-19).

Ed Corley offers some unique insights on the meaning
of Paul's prayer:

The word *strengthened* in Paul's prayer is...from
the Greek *krateo*, a word having to do with government. ...Paul used it in this verse...[speaking] of
the Holy Spirit entering a human spirit, conquering what is wrong, and setting up the new government of Christ's Kingdom. We could translate
Ephesians 3:16 this way: "that you might be
governed with might by His Spirit in the inner
man."

...I believe he meant: "I'm praying for you that the
Holy Spirit will work in your inner man where
there remain areas not yet brought under the
dominion of Christ. These are parts so deep you are
not conscious of them. ... These unconquered parts
allure seducing spirits who desire to take you from
God. My longing, as I hold you in prayer, is that you
will become free from all spiritual defilement so
you can become whole....[7]

Remember that Paul was addressing *Christians* in
this passage! Church leaders who deny that this is possible in Christians are not only incorrect, but will never
lead their people to the inner healing they need!

Lawrence Crabb describes ways we can release the indwelling Christ to glorify Himself:

God is glorified when I bow humbly before Him, ac-
knowledging His right to run my life, and bringing

myself into line with my Creator...I am alive to Him, indwelt by the Holy Spirit, Who works in me "both to do and to will of His good pleasure" (Phil. 2:13). Now each moment of my life...can be seen as part of a larger meaningful whole...my life as a whole and in every detail can intellectually claim to be truly significant as part of the exciting purpose of God Himself.[8]

In other words, a *mature* Christian radiates the presence and preciousness of the Lord to everyone he or she meets, indicating a total abandonment and yieldedness to the indwelling Christ.

3. Inner Heart Healing Now!

Putting aside our interpersonal barriers is perhaps the deepest and most painful of all the workings of the Holy Spirit in our sanctification process. This emphasis on *deep repentance unto inner heart healing* as part of the purging and sanctification process is not just another "fad" of teaching. It is the *most vital issue for serious members of the Body of Christ today*!

The Personal Urgency of Inner Heart Healing

A.W. Tozer describes the powerful grasp of the unrenewed self in his book, *The Pursuit of God*:

Self can live unrebuked at the very altar. It can watch the bleeding Victim die and not be in the least affected by what it sees. It can fight for the faith of the Reformers and preach eloquently the creed of salvation by grace, and gain strength by its efforts. To tell the truth, it seems actually to feed upon orthodoxy and is more at home in a Bible Conference than in a tavern. Our very state of longing after God may afford it an excellent condition under which to thrive and grow.

[But] self is the opaque veil that hides the Face of God from us. It can be removed only in spiritual experience, never by mere instruction. ... There must be a work of God in destruction before we are free. We must invite the cross to do its deadly work within us. We must bring our self-sins to the cross for judgment.[9]

Lawrence Crabb, in his foreword to Dan Allender's book, *The Wounded Heart—Hope For Adult Victims Of Childhood Sexual Abuse*, makes a powerful comment on sanctification as related to inner heart healing:

...the image of God is central to developing a solid view of personality; that our sinfulness, not how we've been sinned against, is our biggest problem; that forgiveness, not wholeness, is our greatest need; that repentance, not insight, is the dynamic in all real change. ...

Nothing matters more than seeing clearly that the gospel of Christ [indeed] speaks with heart-mending compassion and life-changing power to every struggle in life.[10]

This utter depravity of *self* is also still very intrisic to even "spirit-filled" Christians. The sanctifying work of the Holy Spirit is the only solution to life's deepest problems, but it is very painful in its initial stages. Dan Allender warns us:

The process of entering the past will disrupt life or, at least, the existence that masquerades as life. The ease of quiet denial that allows the person to be a pleasant but vacuous doormat or an articulate but driven Bible-study leader will be replaced by tumult, fear, confusion, anger, and change. Marriages will need to be reshaped.... The fabric of life will need to be unraveled piece by piece as the Master reweaves the cloth to His design.

One might wish that the process of sanctification was merely a stroll down a gentle country lane. In fact, the path is through the dark valleys and into the seemingly impenetrable darkness that [at times seems that it] eclipses the light of the Son of God. *The horror of change is that it appears to involve a death that resurrection cannot restore.*

What is the point in pursuing firm hope and lively joy? The answer is simple: to live out the gospel. The reason for entering the struggle is *a desire for more, a taste of what life and love could be if freed from the dark memories and deep shame.*[10]

Allender then discusses the nature, extent, and basis of personal and physical healing through the work of the Holy Spirit today:

First, the work of the Holy Spirit does not lead to sinless perfectionism in this life.... Second, the Holy Spirit's "normal" process of change involves both the dramatic and the mundane. ... Third, the normal work of the Holy Spirit produces crippled warriors who are used *because* of their brokenness, weakness, and powerlessness (1 Corinthians 1:26-29)....

God's path is paradoxical. We are drawn to Christ because we want life, and life more abundant. He gives us life that leads to abundance *via* brokenness, poverty, persecution and death. The life He invites us to lead causes us to lose ourselves so that we can find ourselves, to lose our life so that we can have life. ... The Scriptures promise ultimate health and wealth, but the path to such enjoyment is not what most of us envision or naturally choose.[12]

We can only apply spiritual biblical truths to specific problems if we trust in those truths through the indwelling Christ, and yield to the complex operations of the Holy Spirit. True inner heart healing is a process, and it can only take place as the indwelling Holy Spirit of Christ Jesus deals with our root sins, their embedded emotional empowerments, and their dysfunctional causes in the past.

The Holy Spirit does not lead us to recall past memories to increase our sense of guilt over past sins and failures—in most cases, we merely react to survive. However, the self-protecting goals and strategies we erect for protection from pain quickly become deeply ingrained habits and obstacles to obedient servanthood. We must repent from this form of sin, but *we remain oblivious* to these self-protecting strategies and the hurts they cause *until we make that painful journey into the past* with the Holy Spirit.

Allender points out the threefold purpose for recalling memories of past sinful situations as a starting point for the heart-healing aspect of the sanctification process: "The purpose of regaining memories is threefold: removal of the denial, reclamation of the self, and movement toward real change."[13] This third challenge, "movement toward real change," is the most significant.

Prophetic Timeliness of Inner Heart Healing

I am deeply convinced that the Body of Christ is on the verge of a new move of God, one in which inner heart

106 The Christian Marriage

healing will be a major thrust of our Lord Christ Jesus.[14] God began to pour His Holy Spirit afresh in the late 1980's on many Bible-believing Christians to purify and mature their walk in faith. The primary focus in this purifying and maturing move of God is centered in the apostolic, prophetic, and teaching callings or ministries (including inner heart healing and counseling). It is an overall call to *deep sanctification*. I believe the Body of Christ will be purified during this decade so our Lord Christ Jesus will use this "considerably purified and matured" Body in the most fruitful period of world evangelism in history (while the *parousia* return of our Lord Christ Jesus is yet many decades away)! Indeed, that "fruitful period of world evangelism" will not take place until we are thus purified first.

The sanctification process involves the work of the indwelling Holy Spirit of Christ Jesus dealing with what drives the sins that so easily beset us—our self-seeking, our self-protecting, our self-control, the accompanying embedded emotional empowerments, and anything else outside of our God-ordained call to servanthood. The purpose of the sanctification process is to restore us to that original servanthood.

God is moving on this generation to bring inner heart healing to each of us, purging us of our motives, attitudes, goals, and strategies of self-seeking and self-protecting. This inner heart healing is also a "heart circumcision" that removes the residual barriers to His will. When we are in utter abandonment to Christ, we will be totally entwined with Him so He can at last use us as His love-motivated and Spirit-empowered servants in any way He chooses. He will no longer be constrained by our human limitations and unwillingness. Our sanctification does not end at this point, however; He can now use us as free-flowing vessels through whom He can pour out His light, life, and love.

Inner heart healing directly impacts our maturity as individuals and as a corporate body of believers in three key areas: (a) what or who we are (or our condition and status); (b) our personal relationship with our Lord Christ Jesus; and (c) what we primarily do and how He uses us for His purposes. Here are many elements which I prophetically envision[15] His dealings with His Body during the next few years will involve:

1. What or who we are (or our condition and status):

    a. We are being led through inner heart healing into deep intimacy with our Lord Christ Jesus.

        i.   We are learning to *entwine our lives* with our Lord Christ Jesus (as meant by the phrase, "wait upon" in Isaiah 40:31, King James Version).

        ii. We still tremble in fear at the thought of being totally in the hands of an awesome God (though we love Him).

        iii. The work of His indwelling Holy Spirit continues to deliver us from sins of self-seeking and self-protecting, thus "slipping" us out of self-centeredness.

        iv. Through this He brings inner healing to our hearts.

        v.   We are burying our lusts, as well as our self-seeking, self-protecting desires, goals, and strategies.

        vi. We are being subdued, humbled, and weakened by our trials (though He purifies and strengthens us within).

      vii. He cuts us down and exposes us to our inner depravities, destroying our self-seeking and self-protecting goals and strategies.

      viii. He causes us to set aside all self-seeking and self-protecting behaviors.

  b. We are being driven to Him by overwhelming pressures from the world.

      i. We are narrowly confined by overwhelming circumstances which force us to utterly cling to our Lord.

      ii. Our being buffeted by Satanic forces is stretched out over time, so that the purity of our faith be proven.

      iii. We are being purified and made righteous through our experiences during these purgings.

2. Our personal relationship with Christ in this move:

  a. He is our high priest, acting as our heart circumciser.

      i. The indwelling Holy Spirit of Christ Jesus is inwardly purifying us.

      ii. Even as He inwardly purges us, He holds us tightly as His precious possessions.

      iii. The residual of self is being pushed aside for burial.

      iv. He is our heart circumciser and we are committed to Him for inner heart healing.

  b. We are totally dependent upon Him in all ways.

      i   We live in total dependence upon Him for practically all of our needs.

      ii. The Lord Christ Jesus is making Himself highly visible to us so that we may see Him clearly.

      iii. We glorify Him by freely yielding ourselves to Him in all ways.

      iv. We are totally dependent upon Him for protection, and for providing our identity, purpose, value, significance, and security needs.

  c. We are in a deep love relationship with Him: we know Him and He blesses us in the midst of our humbleness.

      i. Again, in the midst of our healing humiliation (inward purging), He holds us tightly as His precious possessions.

      ii. He has become a close friend and companion as the indwelling Holy Spirit of Christ Jesus.

      iii. We realize that we are highly favored by grace, the indwelling Holy Spirit.

      iv. He approves us as the results of His sanctifying work in our lives.

      v. He continually bestows His grace and blessing on us through His indwelling Holy Spirit.

3. What or who we are (or our condition and status):

  a. We reflect the beauty and preciousness of Christ in our innermost beings.

     i. We more purely reflect His beauty, preciousness, and strength.

     ii. Our hearts are rivers of living waters of God's *rhema* Word. (See John 7:38.)

  b. Hence we attract others to Him.

     i We continually add to the Kingdom of God.

     ii. He uses us to gather in a rich harvest of souls for His Kingdom.

Not by Psychology

Inner heart healing goes far beyond the standard pastoral counseling of the past. Counseling for inner heart healing must go to the roots of what drives sinful behavior. Most pastoral counseling for marriage relationships within "evangelical Christianity" is *impotent* in this area because it relies more on psychology than on the indwelling Holy Spirit of Christ Jesus. It fails to go deep enough to the *roots* of problems and to adequately focus on the *surrender* aspect of the necessary repentance.

Much pastoral counseling focuses on the behavior level. Its goal is to teach each person to recognize destructive or otherwise non-Christian behavior patterns and repent of them (in the sense of determining to forsake them). The problem is that those destructive behavior patterns simply do not go away, unless that counseling (a) goes to the root causes of those destructive behavior patterns (which are almost always accompanied by deeply buried emotional empowerments); and (b) leads the counselee to yield to the Holy Spirit indwelling to bring those emotional empowerments to the surface so they can be surrendered to Christ.

Flesh cannot fight flesh, nor self fight self; we must allow Christ to remove underlying emotional empowerments. Trying to stop such behavior merely with "determined discipline" is like trying to squash a partly inflated balloon—if it is pushed down in one place, it will only bulge out at another!

Modern psychological approaches are impotent in helping most Christians in need of inner heart healing for the following five specific reasons:

1. Modern psychological approaches are based on an erroneous model or concept of the human psychological makeup. We are body, soul, and spirit, not id, ego, and libido. (Incidentally, most of the original theories of Freud, including Jung's interpretations, have been scientifically proven in recent decades to be false.)

   We were created for servanthood, and our human spirits "need" both a means of serving and others to receive our servanthood. But due to the Fall, we vainly strive to meet those needs by self-seeking. The result is deep-seated frustrations. Since modern psychology denies this, its counseling fails to deal with the root issues of our heart illnesses and hurts. At best, they can only temporarily alleviate some of the symptoms.

2. Modern psychological approaches have the erroneous goal of achieving "happiness," rather than *full inner heart healing*. Our relationship with Christ, our Tree of Life (our source of oneness with God, our needed fulfillment, and our sought-for acceptance), is the real essence and goal of true life fulfillment. Counseling approaches *based on secular psychology* and "happiness" can

at best provide only interim relief of some of the pain we feel.

3. Modern psychological approaches are incapable of dealing with the root issues of human need. Biblical counseling requires *repentance,* a concept that is foreign to modern psychology. Even most Christians misunderstand repentance. Repentance must be specific to be effective in inner heart healing. It must be specific in its form, or in *how* we "repent" (we must fully *surrender all* unto Christ). We must know *what* must specifically be surrendered to Christ, and we must repent and surrender it for the proper reason.

4. Modern psychological approaches to counseling are doomed to fail because they deny the vital role of the indwelling Holy Spirit of Christ Jesus in inner heart healing. Specifically, they deny the work of the Holy Spirit in counselors to help them discern the root issues in the hurting Christian, and to empower the counselee to repent and receive full inner heart healing.

5. Modern psychology denies the role of demons and their amplification of darkness in human thought life. "Darkness" means absence of the light of Christ indwelling. Demons are attracted to darkness, and they usually amplify the embedded emotional empowerments within us that are associated with that darkness. Such demonic activity is easily abated by the Name of Jesus Christ and the power of the Holy Spirit.

Let me continue on this last point. When demonic reinforcement of dark thought patterns is strong, we cannot expect victory through counseling psychology—*even as practiced within Christianity.* Modern psychology, being a "heuristic" science, has discovered many techniques that indeed work on a superficial level, but are helpless in dealing with demonic influences! Rebecca Brown, M.D., for example, emphasizes this fact in cases of dysfunctionally-rooted problems arising out of child abuse:

> Many Christians are getting on the band wagon to set up organizations to publicize the problem of ritualistic abuse of children [or other forms of dysfunctionalism] and supposedly to help parents and victims. However, they are refusing [or failing] to take a firm stand for Christ and are trying to approach this problem on a strictly secular basis, working with governmental agencies in most cases. They are all doomed to fail miserably! Why? Because this is spiritual warfare and can only be dealt with by clearly recognizing that the problem[s] involve[s] spiritual forces. Demons can only be dealt with [by] the power and authority of Jesus Christ. Psychology is completely helpless to do anything with demons. [16]

This problem has concerned pastors and other Christian ministers for many years. Pastoral counseling directly addresses it. The "nouthetic counseling" approach of Jay Adams[17] has been widely practiced now for more than 20 years, although I have observed widespread misuse of this approach to counseling (apart from the vital work of the Holy Spirit), with much destruction of faith in otherwise genuine Christians. Many exorcism ministries have arisen as Christian counselors recognized the demonic activity in such inner problems. Of course, secular psychiatrists, following several counseling approaches, are widely available. All of these attest to some success, and that is wonderful. But none have success rates anywhere near approaching that which we would expect with Christ Himself available to us Christians!

Rather, Christian counselors are to serve by helping to restore "communication" between the counselee and the Lord during those times when personal issues and emotions have "messed up" his/her faith. They are not there to play psychological games. A good counselor also helps to enhance communication between spouses in marriage counseling. In all cases, the counselor's role is not to "play God," to judge anyone, to batter anyone with Scripture, or to humiliate or embarrass anyone.

Throwing Out the Baby With the Bath Water

Although many Bible-believing and "Spirit-filled" Christians strongly reject modern psychological counseling approaches as unbiblical (including most forms of Christian pastoral counseling), we urge caution. Although it is correct to reject these approaches in some important ways, it also throws out "some important babies with the bath water."

Intensive counseling is required for inner heart healing in most cases. While we vigorously toss out the majority of the assumptions and methods of modern psychology, we must avoid losing the tremendous insights that Christian counselors have discovered. These are of great help when exercising the ministry of discerning of spirits during counseling. We address here not the erroneous theoretical foundations of psychology, but rather the practical guidelines and insights that have been proven in practical experience by Christian counselors anointed by the indwelling Holy Spirit of Christ Jesus. They share their life experiences with us in many excellent books that have become available to us since the late 1980's.

Secular psychology has been trying to address dysfunctionally-rooted issues in troubled people under different terms under non-biblical models of the human psychological makeup; however, limited success has been possible by the *empirical nature* of the discipline.

For example, Abraham Maslow's classical theory lists five human needs:

1. *Physical* needs (of the physical body to live),

2. Physical *security*,

3. *Love* (Crabb calls this "security"[18,19]),

4. *Purpose* (Crabb calls this "significance"[20,21]), and

5. *Self-actualization* (development into a full, creative, self-expressing person).

Lawrence Crabb notes that these "needs" actually reflect the biblical model of the human psychological makeup to a certain extent:

> ...security or love is a more basic need than purpose or significance. However, both are required before I will be motivated to truly express who I am, simply because until I enjoy security and significance, I do not believe I really am anyone.

> ...Maslow's third and fourth needs (love and purpose) correspond to what I call the personal needs [or deepest longings] of man: security and significance. Self-actualization ... comes close to the Biblical concept of becoming mature in Christ....

> ...the personal needs [deepest longings] of significance and security can be fully met only in a relationship with a personal God. It therefore follows that only a Christian has the resources to become truly self-actualized. ... If personal needs

[deepest longings] can be met only in a relationship with a personal God [Christ indwelling], then only a Christian has the resources to reach the fifth stage, to actualize himself, and therefore to be truly well-adjusted.[22]

Even this thinking is more self-centered than Christ-centered. The last three, not just the third and fourth, *come only* through our choosing to allow Christ in us to flow forth. *A Christian can never "actualize" himself.* Only by the indwelling Christ flowing in and through us is self-actualization (in this sense) actually experienced. The richest goal we can possibly reach in this life is the deep satisfaction that comes from knowing that we have done and are doing the right things—and only Christ indwelling can give us that wisdom and assurance!

4. A New Age Smokescreen

Satan has established, through the modern secular psychological "self-help recovery" movement, a "smokescreen" that confuses and deceives many today, including sincere Christians. A "smokescreen" is a tactic satan uses when he cannot directly attack a biblical truth that is too deeply ingrained in Christian thinking, or too important to Christians for them to believe his lies about. So he takes that truth and expands it out of proportion, removes parallel biblical truths (such as that of the workings of the Holy Spirit of Christ dwelling in a Christian's human spirit), and adds subtle lies. Thus he not only entices many weak believers and non-believers, but also intimidates Christians from teaching on the biblical concept itself. A classic example is the Jehovah's Witnesses emphasis on "the Kingdom of God." That certainly is a biblical truth—Jesus spoke much on it—that they have expanded in worldly terms and purged of the parallel truth of the divinity of Christ. So many have been deceived into the movement. But also, when was the last time you heard a true Christian explanation of what Jesus actually meant by "the Kingdom of God?"

My deep concern is to identify the core biblical truths underlying our needs for inner heart healing, put them back into biblical context, and direct the sincere Christian to walk in Christ in faith in those biblical truths. Over the years the psychologists have indeed phenomenologically observed *something*. Regardless of how they interpreted it, it is basically a form of *self*ishness (and hence sin) based on one's seeking need-fulfillment by self-efforts rather than from Christ, and rather than walking in love-motivated servanthood, which requires loss of self. As sin, it can be dealt with only through repentance (a repentance involving surrender) of it and one's root needs, to Christ. Without that "surrender-repentance," it wreaks havoc in virtually *all* Christian marriage relationships!

Our need for inner heart healing is a vital, root biblical truth that we dare not allow satan to smokescreen. That biblical inner heart healing involves at least three steps: (a) seeking and cooperating with the indwelling Holy Spirit to search out our hearts, (i.e., to bring our self-seeking and self-protecting to our cognitive awareness); (b) surrender-repenting of it, and its accompanying emotional empowerments, unto Christ at Calvary where He takes away our sins, iniquities, and sicknesses; and (c) embracing Christ not just as Savior and Lord, but as our Tree of Life that satisfies the root needs of our human spirits which our self-efforts try in vain to meet.

I do severely fault both sides of the argument between the "New Age" psychologists and the evangelical Christians who oppose it, but along lines that neither have mentioned so far. The latter try to argue about what are truly *spiritual* phenomena, needs, or issues, by purely intellectual means. The result would be laughable if it were not so serious a matter. This situation is historically understandable. Since early in the second century A.D. the "Western" world, including "Christianity," has been captive to the ancient Greek philosophies (particularly neo-Platonism and Stoicism). These teach that we humans are "body and soul" (but not also spirit), and that understanding anything of a "spiritual" nature means high theological doctrine. As a result, almost all forms of Christianity today fail to grasp the elementary concepts of Jesus' teaching that (a) He is Spirit, (b) worship of Him is in the Spirit, (c) we must become born again in our (human) spirits, (d) His Holy Spirit dwells in and works through our (human) spirits once we become born again, and (e) His purpose for us (i.e., "sanctification") is to become Lord of us by our allowing Him to rule us through His Holy Spirit, specifically by our (our souls) yielding to Him in us.

In the meantime, the recent major influence of "Eastern mystic" religions (which recognize the reality of "spiritual" things) in the "Western" world, has given rise to the force of the "New Age" religion and so has "spiritualized" secular psychology. Christians, who should have a much deeper and more powerful grasp on spiritual reality, are horribly impotent to deal with New Agers who daily experience spiritual phenomena.

End Notes: Chapter Five

1. McGee, Robert S. *The Search For Significance* (Houston, TX: Published by the author, 1987).

2. Joyner, Rick. *The Harvest* (Pineville, NC: Morning-Star Publications, 1989), p. 53.

3. Munroe, Myles. *In Pursuit of Purpose* (Shippensburg, PA: Destiny Image Publishers, 1992), Preface.

4. Wilkerson, David. *Have You Felt Like Giving Up Lately?* (Tarrytown, NY: Spire Books, Fleming H. Revell Co., 1980), p. 40.

5. We *know* it is God's will for our marriages to be healed and enriched.

6. Maxwell, L.E. *Born Crucified* (Chicago, IL: Moody Press, 1945, rev. ed. 1973), pp. 16,21,23. Copyright © 1945 by Moody Bible Institute of Chicago. Used by permission.

7. Corley, Ed. "The Human Spirit—Dumping Ground of the Emotions." *Maschil*, June-July 1990, (a publication of the Berean Gospel Fellowship, P.O. Box 667, Lincolnton, GA 30817-0667), p. 2.

8. Crabb, Lawrence J., Jr. *Basic Principles of Biblical Counseling* (Grand Rapids, MI: Zondervan Publishing House, 1975), p. 58. Copyright © 1975 by Zondervan

Publishing House. Used by permission of Zondervan Publishing House.

9. Tozer, A.W. *The Pursuit of God* (Harrisburg, PA: Christian Publications, Inc., 1948), 1982 edition, pp. 45-46.

10. Allender, Dan. *The Wounded Heart—Hope For Adult Victims Of Childhood Sexual Abuse* (Colorado Springs, CO: NavPress, 1990). Copyright © 1990 by Dr. Dan B. Alldender. Used by permission of NavPress. All rights reserved. For copies, call 1-800-366-7788.

11. Allender. *The Wounded Heart*, pp. 26-27.

12. Allender. *The Wounded Heart*, pp. 142-143.

13. Allender. *The Wounded Heart*, p. 186.

14. See Sherrerd, Chris S. *From Sheepfold to Bride: Christ Maturing His Church*, Vol. III of the series, "Where Do You Fit In? Practical Commitments in the Body of Christ" (to be published).

15. Sherrerd. *From Sheepfold to Bride.*

16. Brown, Rebecca, M.D. *Prepare For War* (Springs-dale, PA: Whitaker House, 1987), p. 210. Used by permission of the publisher, Whitaker House, 580 Pittsburgh Street, Springsdale, PA 15144.

17. Adams, Jay E. *Competent to Counsel* (Grand Rapids, MI: Baker Book House, 1970). See also Jay E. Adams, *Coping With Counseling Crises—First Aid for Christian Counselors* (Grand Rapids, MI: Baker Book House, 1976).

18. Crabb, Lawrence J., Jr. *Effective Biblical Counseling* (Grand Rapids, MI: Ministry Resources Library, Zondervan Publishing House, 1977). Copyright © 1977 by

The Zondervan Corporation. Used by permission of Zondervan Publishing House.

19. Crabb, Lawrence J., Jr. *Understanding People—Deep Longings for Relationship* (Grand Rapids, MI: Ministry Resourses Library, Zondervan Publishing House, 1987).

20. Crabb, *Effective Biblical Counseling.* Copyright © 1977 by The Zondervan Corporation. Used by permission of Zondervan Publishing House.

21. Crabb. *Understanding People.*

22. Crabb, Lawrence J. *Effective Biblical Counseling,* pp. 79-81. Copyright © 1977 by The Zondervan Corporation. Used by permission of Zondervan Publishing House.

Chapter Six

Biblical Portraits of Inner Heart Healing

To the best of my knowledge, the phrase *inner heart healing* was originally coined by this author. However, several of the concepts associated with inner heart healing have familiar biblical types and meanings that provide deep insights. These include:

1. Cleansing from all unrighteousness (see 1 John 1:9).

2. Heart circumcision (see Rom. 2:29).

3. Circumcising "soul-spirit barriers" by the Word of God (see Heb. 4:12).

4. Plowing fallow ground (see Jer. 4:3-4; Hos. 10:12).

5. Tearing down thought strongholds (see 2 Cor. 10:4-5).

6. Coming out of darkness (see 1 Pet. 2:9).

7. Deep calling to deep (see Ps. 42:7-8).

1. Cleansing Us From All Unrighteousness

If we confess our sins, He is faithful and righteous to forgive us our sins and to cleanse us from all un-righteousness (1 John 1:9).

Most Bible-believing Christians are familiar with Scripture passages on basic salvation such as John 3:16, etc. Most know they have been "saved" in the sense of their eternal destiny. But how about the many sins that still *so easily beset us* (Heb. 12:1 KJV)? The majority of true believers still struggle with sin, many years after their initial "salvation!" They wonder (in a form of dis-belief) if they haven't long since "worn out" First John 1:9, since they have sinned and confessed so many times. God's patience with us is long-suffering—but for how long?

The passage in First John 1:9 tells us we are cleansed of what drives us to sin so easily in the same basic way as forgiveness: *by confession* and *repentance.* This includes agreeing with God that these things are sins, and by fol-lowing all of the biblical steps of repentance. This process is closely tied to the Old Testament concept of atonement expressed in the Hebrew word *KPhR,* which means "to render powerless." That is exactly what the indwelling Holy Spirit of Christ Jesus does to our *embedded emo-tions.* It "renders them powerless" to drive our sinful be-havior patterns during our inner heart healing!

2. Heart Circumcision

But he is a Jew [of Judah] *who is one inwardly; and circumcision is that which is of the heart, by the Spirit, not by the letter; and his praise is not from men, but from God* (Romans 2:29).

Look closely at the *details* in this passage. *Circum-cision* is an *inward act* of the heart! Identification with

Judah (which means "praise") is done *inwardly*, and everything is done *by the [Holy] Spirit*, not by the letter of the law or by men.

What is "heart circumcision"? This is a biblical type, which is a tool used by the Holy Spirit to help us understand spiritual truths in the Scriptures. Things of *spiritual reality* (i.e., things pertaining to the spiritual domain, especially of the Godhead) are beyond the capabilities of our natural mind and understanding—we are unable to directly and readily grasp them apart from God. God carefully ordained natural events and recordings in His written Word to be "object lessons" to help us understand spiritual truths.

First Corinthians 15:46 gives us the basic principle of biblical types by comparing the "first" Adam with Christ (the second Adam): "However, the spiritual is not first, but the natural; then the spiritual" (1 Cor. 15:46). First the natural; then the spiritual—that's the principle. One of many scriptural examples of this valuable teaching tool is found in John 10:7 and 10:9, where Jesus describes Himself as a "doorway" or means of entering into eternal life. The Book of Hebrews also contains many biblical types relating Old Testament ceremonial law and the tabernacle in the wilderness to Christ and His relationship with His Body today.

Romans 2:29, using the Old Testament law of circumcision as a type, is yet another example. It is referred to in both Testaments as a type. Deuteronomy 10:16 says, "Circumcise then your heart, and stiffen your neck no more." Deuteronomy 30:6 says, "...God will circumcise your heart...to love the Lord your God with all your heart and with all your soul, in order that you may live." Jeremiah 4:4 continues, "Circumcise yourselves to the Lord and remove the foreskins of your heart...." Romans 2:28-29 says, "But he is a Jew [of Judah] who is one inwardly; and circumcision is that which is of the heart, by the Spirit...and his praise is...from God." According to Romans 4:9-12, circumcision is a seal or outward sign that the righteousness of God is already in us. Romans 15:8-12 shows that Christ's circumcision makes all, Jews or Gentiles, children of the Abrahamic promises. Philippians 3:3 says, "for we are the true circumcision, who worship in the Spirit of God and glory in Christ Jesus and put no confidence [trust] in the flesh." Colossians 2:11 states, "And in Him [Christ] you were also circumcised with a circumcision made without hands, in the removal of the body of the flesh by the circumcision of Christ."

Old Testament circumcision involved a deliberate cutting of physical flesh by a high priest. The Hebrew verb for "circumcise," *MWL*, means "to cut into or away." The New Testament Greek equivalent, *peritemno*, specifically means "to cut around or to inscribe around." Under the Old Covenant, this cutting was a prerequisite for entering into certain covenants with God. Genesis 17:11-14, 26-27 notes Abraham's circumcision of Ishmael, and Genesis 21:4 and Acts 7:8 record Abraham's circumcision of Isaac.

Circumcision was emphasized as a "cutting out to be separate" or a "cutting to mark or designate as belonging to God." In Leviticus 12:3, circumcision was prescribed as part of the Mount Sinai (or Mount Horeb) covenant law. It was also mentioned as a prerequisite to Passover (*PSCh*) in Exodus 12:43-48. It was required for a subsequent or mature walk in the Lord before entering into ministry in Exodus 4:24-26, and no uncircumcised man could enter into warfare to overcome and possess the Promised Land according to Joshua 5:2-7.

The Old Testament history of the Israelites actually mentions *two circumcisions*—the circumcision of the covenant of Passover (see Ex. 12:43-48, see also Gen. 17:4-16); and that of embarking on conquering the Promised Land (see Josh. 5:2-7). The first is associated with deliverance, and it typifies regeneration, when we come into communication with God through our human spirits and learn of Him. This inward circumcision is a vital part of our entrance into covenant relationship with God, and God "marking" us as His own.

The second circumcision is associated with the beginning of a walk in the power of the presence of God. It typifies the baptism into the Holy Spirit.

At that time the Lord said to Joshua, "Make for yourself flint knives and circumcise again the sons of Israel the second time." So Joshua made himself flint knives and circumcised the sons of Israel at Gibeath-haaraloth ["the hill of the foreskins"]. *And this is the reason why Joshua circumcised them: all the people who came out of Egypt who were males, all the men or war, died in the wilderness along the way, after they came out of Egypt. For all the people who came out were circumcised, but all the people who were born in the wilderness along the way as they came out of Egypt had not been circumcised. For the sons of Israel walked forty years in the wilderness, until all the nation, that is, the men of war who came out of Egypt, perished because they did not listen to the voice of the Lord, to whom the Lord had sworn that He would not let them see the land which the Lord had sworn to their fathers to give us, a land flowing with milk and honey. And their children whom He raised up in their place, Joshua circumcised; for they were uncircumcised, because they had not circumcised them along the way* (Joshua 5:2-7).

But what does it mean it circumcise our "hearts"? That we now discuss.

3. The Word of God Circumcising Our Soul-Spirit Barriers

Hebrews 4:12 refers to the "barriers of the heart": "For the [*rhema*] word of God is living and active and sharper than any two-edged sword, and piercing as far as the division of soul and spirit, of both joints [bone] and marrow, and able to judge the thoughts and intentions of the heart."

The function of the high priest to cut or inscribe the "foreskin" of the male organ used to "disperse the seed of life" in Old Covenant circumcision is a powerful *New Covenant type of heart circumcision*. That cutting, though quite painful for a moment, renders the male organ more sensitive to physical stimuli. This ceremony was done by the high priest under the Mosaic Law. Before the Aaronic order of priesthood was specifically established, the patriarch (Abraham) or leader of Israel (Moses and Joshua) administered this rite.

In our anti-type, our High Priest (Christ Jesus), wields the knife of the dynamic Word of God to inscribe or cut away the soul's grip over the redeemed human spirit. Our human spirits are the "male organs" that He uses to disperse the seed of Eternal Life. Our souls become sensitive and responsive to the indwelling Holy Spirit of Christ Jesus as He deals with us through our human spirits.

Our High Priest cuts away the *barrier of control* that our wills hold over our behavior—our barriers of self-seeking and self-protecting, and our barriers of insensitivity to God's will. The knife is the Word of God (*rhema* or dynamic dealings of God in our lives by His Holy Spirit). His objective is to "cut" our motives, thoughts, and wills to help them become sensitive to His flowing out of us to others. When Christ in us can flow out to others freely as He wills, unhindered by self, then He may freely disperse the seed of Eternal Life *through us* to a sin-weary world.

Heart circumcision involves more than the soul's "allowing the spirit" to commune with God; it involves the soul's yielding to the influence and control of the indwelling Holy Spirit. That means releasing self-consciousness beyond self, beyond personal control, unto the lordship of Christ. We grow from being servants or bondslaves of Christ to being vessels that literally contain Him and to being instruments used by Him. Self-seeking and even self-consciousness are set aside. It is one of the most drastic of all forms of repentance we must take.

Before this circumcision of the heart occurs, as long as the "self" or soul dominates that spirit organ, the human spirit is totally impotent (even though we may be filled with the Holy Spirit and contain Him and the righteousness of God). Christ chooses to not override our wills; He allows our souls to dominate. However, when we choose to yield to Him and to release self (our souls) to Him, then He allows His Holy Spirit to function through our behavior and attitudes according to His will. Thus we become "those of the true circumcision," the true children of the Abrahamic promise, the true Israel in regal relationship with God.

This is clearly depicted in the life of Abraham (see Gen. 17). Like Abraham, when we take matters in our own hand and strive through our own efforts outside of our "rest in Christ," all things seem to fail. Finally, we are driven to deeply seek the Lord, at all costs. We get into our prayer closets and stay there until He answers, "I am *El Shaddai* (*AL ShDY*; literally, 'your almighty nursing breast'); come close to Me."

The Bible presents even more pictures of this in the many references to dwelling in a "wilderness" (i.e., a "wilderness walk with Him"). The issue is that we are forced to be *utterly dependent* upon Him for everything— we are totally helpless otherwise.

4. Plowing Fallow Ground

Another biblical type of inner heart healing is revealed in the phrase, *plowing fallow ground.*

> *For thus says the Lord to the men of Judah and to Jerusalem,* **"Break up your fallow ground,** *and do not sow among thorns. Circumcise yourselves to the Lord, and remove the foreskins of your heart..."* (Jeremiah 4:3-4).

> *Sow with a view to righteousness, reap in accordance with kindness;* **break up your fallow ground,** *for it is time to seek the Lord until He comes to rain righteousness on you* (Hosea 10:12).

Look closely at the elements of this biblical picture and type:

1. "Fallow ground" in the Hebrew (*NYR*) means "that which has already been plowed or tilled."

2. To plow deeply is to bring roots to the surface.

3. The "foreskins of the heart" are related to heart circumcision.

4. The phrase *to righteousness* is related to First John 1:9.

5. We are to do it unto the Lord.

6. We are to sow and reap righteousness and compassion.

7. We are to seek the Lord.

This purging, cleansing, and plowing of the Holy Spirit is plowing a *second time*, a deeper uprooting of things left untouched the first time. It is a cleansing of unrighteousness which was not dealt with upon initial "salvation." Thus it is yet another reference to heart circumcision in those who are already Christians.

5. Tearing Down Thought Strongholds

For the weapons of our warfare are not of the flesh, but divinely powerful for the destruction of fortresses [Greek: *topon*]. *We are destroying speculations and every lofty thing raised up against the knowledge of God, and we are taking every thought captive to the obedience of Christ* (2 Corinthians 10:4-5).

God calls Christians to destroy "fortresses" or strongholds of speculation, and to do it through mental discipline, "taking every thought captive to the obedience of Christ."

Ephesians 4:27 is a parallel passage that exhorts us to "not give the devil an opportunity." The Greek word for "opportunity" is *topon/topos*, which means "a place marked off with boundaries, an area of legal jurisdiction." It refers to a "place" in our souls where satan has a *legal right to rule* because we have *given* him permission to do so. This includes any area in our thought-lives in which we give him a foothold.

We need healing from these *topon* areas in our thought-lives, these strongholds of satan. But this healing can only come through deep surrender-repentance, as we "dump" these onto Christ in the inner heart healing process.

6. Coming Out of Darkness

Darkness is another powerful biblical portrait of these *topon* "strongholds of satan" in our thought-lives. It is best illustrated in First Peter 2:9: "But you are a chosen race, a royal priesthood, a holy nation, a people for God's own possession, that you may proclaim the excellencies of Him who has called you out of darkness into His marvelous light."

Many other Scripture passages clearly identify "ways of darkness" with ways of evil, of unrighteousness, of dwelling in satan's "world" (*kosmos*); whereas "light" is identified as the life of Christ. For example, Proverbs 2:13-14 speaks of "those who leave the paths of uprightness, to walk in the ways of darkness; who delight in doing evil, and rejoice in the perversity of evil."

The Gospel of John tells us that light is the life of Jesus, and darkness is the way of the world and hence of evil under satan (see Jn. 1:4-5; 3:19-20; 8:12; 12:35,46). Acts 26:18 links darkness to the dominion of satan (*kosmos* or "world"), and light to God and our source of forgiveness of sins. Romans 13:12 says, "...Let us therefore lay aside the deeds of darkness and put on the armor of light." Second Corinthians 6:14 links righteousness to light and lawlessness to darkness. Ephesians 5:11 admonishes us to "not participate in the unfruitful deeds of darkness, but instead even expose them." Ephesians 6:12 links satan's domain to the world forces of darkness. Colossians 1:13 reads: "for He [the Father] delivered us from the domain of darkness, and transferred us to the kingdom of His beloved Son [Jesus]."

First Thessalonians 5:4-8 again links the kingdom of darkness to being without Christ in satan's world (*kosmos*), and walking in the ways of light as "sons of the day" to living in Christ. First John 1:5 says, "...God is light, and in Him there is no darkness at all." Verse 6 continues to warn us that if we walk in darkness, we have no fellowship with Him. First John 2:11 links hatred with darkness: "But the one who hates his brother is in the darkness and walks in the darkness, and...the darkness has blinded his eyes."

Most of these Scripture passages are addressed to Christians, to those already in Christ. Darkness means without light, or in this case, "without the life of Christ." Darkness in these passages means almost the same thing as the *topon* "strongholds" of satan in our thought lives. They must be healed by deep surrender-repentance in inner heart healing.

What about demons in all of this? Since demons are attracted to darkness, we must focus on the darkness, not on demons. If we expose the darkness to the light of Christ, then they will flee.

7. Deep Calleth to Deep

Deep calls to deep at the sound of Thy waterfalls; all Thy breakers and Thy waves have rolled over me. The Lord will command His lovingkindness in the daytime; and His song will be with me in the night, a prayer to the God of my life (Psalm 42:7-8).

Let the breakers and waves of "strongholds" of darkness (the inner psychological "hang-ups," secret sins, and relational problems) rise to the surface of cognitive awareness, so that through prayer they will be replaced by His lovingkindness.

8. Summary of These Biblical Portraits

Biblical inner heart healing carries the following ideas:

1.   Jesus as our High Priest

2.   Works His Holy Spirit in us

3.   In painful ways of cleansing

4.   To expose and remove deep roots of things unrighteous

5.   Or cuts to remove barriers

6.   Or "strongholds" of satan in our thought lives.

7.   Or areas of darkness in our behavior patterns

8.   Which run deep

9.   And which hinder His will and full righteousness in us.

Ultimate victory requires our conscious, deliberate, and persistent choice to handle our inner sense of emptiness and worthlessness solely by dynamic faith in *Christ in us*. Our active choice is crucial because it is the only way to release the power of the indwelling Christ. Since our sovereign God has chosen to never work against our human wills, then as long as our human wills are contrary to His, He will not act. When *we do* align our wills with His, then He is quick to *empower* us to live victoriously and to fulfill our destiny. He will even act to nullify evil thought patterns and influences from satan and his demonic forces.

Inner heart healing exposes every unclean sin and promotes cleansing and healing repentance of everything that hinders our Christlike walk. Everything that hinders us from Christlikeness is darkness. These things become strongholds of satan in our thought life if we allow him in. They do not necessarily begin as sins *per se*, but they usually lead to sinful behavior. Our repentance must be specific in form as well as in content. We must surrender to Christ on Calvary because He hung there to take away our sins and our sicknesses as our "scapegoat."

Chapter Seven

Roots in Inner Heart Healing

Before any of us can become whole, the Holy Spirit of Jesus Christ must cut, plow, rile up, and probe deeply into the *roots* of our unrighteousnesses, most of which are in the 90 percent that is below the surface of our cognitive awareness. Only when we become aware of them can we exercise our will to dump these things onto Christ at Calvary.

As we discussed in the preceding chapter, the Bible offers hints and references to these "roots" in several ways:

> All *unrighteousnesses* to be cleansed from us;
> *Foreskin* of our heart to be cut;
> *Soul-spirit barriers* to be removed;
> *Thoughts and intents of the heart* to be discerned;
> Areas of *darkness* to be exposed to light; and
> Inner heart *sicknesses* to be healed.

Only Christ (our Tree of Life) within us can satisfy our root needs. Although most Christians don't realize it, the appropriation of Christ as the Tree of Life involves far more than simply appropriating Him as Savior, Lord, and

Head of His Body. We must also appropriate Him as our High Priest and "Heart Circumciser," as "He who wields the sharp knife" of the *rhema* Word of God (see Heb. 4:12). This is the way our Lord uproots, exposes, and removes every root of our guilt and shame, and every "encumbrance" that hinders His will in our lives.

One of the most difficult lessons of faith to learn is that true joy comes when we yield to His purgings, when we surrender to Him all that does not please Him. As we do this, we will learn that He, our High Priest and Heart Circumciser, is a marvelous God of love!

But until we learn to release Christ in us in everyday life and experience, we will remain empty and unfulfilled. Inner heart healing can come only as we discover and reverse the wrong inner choices (usually subconscious) we have made to resist His will. This is the real meaning of "repentance"; the way we truly "walk in faith." Until then, the monster of *self* remains on the throne of our lives, existing in deception and darkness *separate* from the indwelling Christ.

1. Our Inner Voids and Deepest Longings

The "bottom line" is that our deep inner hurts, "hang-ups," and secret sins are rooted in our failure to *choose to yield* to the indwelling Christ at the "deepest required level" of our beings.

What is that "deepest required level"? It is that of our human *spirits*. To the same extent that we fail to yield to Christ's life in and through us, we will find that our human spirits are hollow inner cores, with the intended functions of the human spirit unfulfilled (yearning, longing, love, wisdom, significance). We have already noted that the human spirit has specific needs that must be filled outside of "self" in order for us to function as God intends as *love-motivated* servants. These needs fall into three categories: the need to be loved, accepted, and secure; the need to have a sense of significance, purpose, and value; and the need to have others receive our servanthood.

We also examined the pattern that emerged under the Adamic curse, as man sought in vain to find *fulfillment of these needs* through *self-seeking* efforts to manipulate others. Most of us unfairly expect our spouses or other people to fulfill those needs. But God never intended or equipped them for this task. This inevitably produces intense and seemingly life-threatening disappointments. This pattern generates the most excruciating emotional pain known to the human race—a pain so intense that we cannot cope with it without denying it, covering it up, or diverting that emptiness with all sorts of self-protecting goals and strategies.

2. A Christian's Sandwiched Soul

Our Creator, in His infinite wisdom, created us with incredible capabilities in our human spirits. There are two ways our human spirits can be "plunged" into dynamic spiritual reality, and the Christian's soul is caught in a tug-of-war between the two. The first (and most desirable) route is by totally yielding the human spirit to the indwelling Holy Spirit of Christ Jesus. This requires continuous, conscious, and deliberate acts of the will (i.e., soul) to invite Him in and to yield to His lordship in all areas. The second route of human spirit activation is that of self-seeking—seeking to live through the efforts of "self." Countless souls are being enticed to discover this route through various New Age means and related practices.

Every person's "self," or soul, is sandwiched between two strong opposing forces: the indwelling Holy Spirit of

Christ Jesus, and the dark thoughts that are deeply ingrained in our habitual patterns of self-seeking and protection from inner pains. Oh, what wretched and torn people we are (see Rom. 7:24)!

The soul—the seat of "self"—is trapped in the middle of a cosmic conflict portrayed by Paul in Romans 7:14-25, a conflict that is primarily waged in our thoughts. Thoughts have power—power to either release Christ in us or to keep us in bondage. We cannot actually live the life of the indwelling Christ as long as our thoughts remain conditioned by our habitual patterns of self-seeking fulfillment, and as long as we try to satisfy the demands of our carnality and soulishness with behavior that is not Christ-centered.

Christians think thoughts from three sources: (a) the indwelling Holy Spirit of Christ ("My sheep hear My voice" [Jn. 10:27]), speaking through our intuition and conscience during praise, worship, prayer, or meditation upon God's written Word; (b) our world-conditioned mind with its habitual patterns of self-seeking (the Bible calls it the "vain and foolish imaginations of our heart" [Rom. 1:21 paraphrased]); and (c) satan the deceiver.

Writer Ed Corley noted:

> ...many...have inner hurts. Frequently they are persons who have received Christ, attended church and listened to sermons for years. Some are believers committed to serving the Lord—but with a satanic darkness gnawing at their inner man. Of course, this is often suppressed, in some more than in others. But one need only scratch beneath the surface of just about anyone to find spiritual ill. Buried inside are the things of which we tell, like rejection, resentment, insecurity, hatred, guilt, and

lust. Often these go so far back in a life the person has forgotten the actual incidents that planted them there.

Many holding inward hurts and filth overcome them to the point of maintaining an outward cool, or religious air—so long as no one touches their "sore spot." The trouble is, someone is always touching that sore spot.[1]

Inner spiritual healing is a prevailing need for all Christians. This need places two requirements on every individual member of the Body of Christ: (a) to recognize our personal needs and take initiatives to be healed and set free ourselves; and (b) to function in Christian love according to our individual callings to assist our brothers and sisters in their inner heart healings. A *breaking* may be required to bring us to the humiliating realization that we each need that inner heart healing walk so we can be plunged into Christ's lordship over our *total* self.

We have not yet learned to plead the shed blood of Jesus over the carnality, the phobias, and the obsessions that often plague our lives. We have not yet learned the difference between laboring *for* the Lord and laboring *with* Him—that is why we experience "burnout" without fulfillment. We cling to false expectations of what our Lord is doing in our lives, and so waste energy and time in vain pursuits.

3. The Human Spirit as a Dumping Ground

Ed Corley provides some excellent insights on how the human spirit is a dumping ground of these many dark thoughts—even in true Bible-believing Christians. He also describes how the indwelling Holy Spirit of Christ seeks to set us free:

The human spirit, with amazing power to control, operates from beneath the level of mental consciousness. ... It is the part most desired by the Lord, and at the same time most sought after by the devil. It is the control room of a life and bears the weight of one's personality. It gives direction to the way a person thinks and acts. And, it dictates how one reacts toward others.

...many people are in trouble. They have stored in them [their spirits] their life's hurts. This is especially so of traumas the emotions can't handle for very long—like the trauma of sexual molestation, the pain of a marriage failing and a home breaking up, the grief that comes from the death of a loved one, the horror of a serious illness, the shock of rejection by a friend, the loss of a job, and so on. ...

The [human] spirit is also where fears and hatred are stored. It is where moral uncleanness and lust hide, awaiting the opportune moment to send their signals to the mind and emotions. [It]...is the depository for resentment and bitterness. While the [human] spirit can also be a depository for good things [i.e., love] it is usually the bad that gets shoved inside its delicate walls. Good things are kept nearer to the surface of the mind. ...

How does defilement get into the [human] spirit? It often comes in youth. Early shocks and emotional upheavals take their toll. Rejection, perhaps more than any other trauma, leaves many...disabled.... With the prevalence of sexual abuse, many children are wounded inwardly and grow into adults with all kinds of spiritual, emotional, mental, and physical disorders. ...

Rejection [perhaps the most common defilement among Christians as well as others today], particularly when it comes from a parent, wounds a child's spirit. Throughout life he continues hearing, "I'm not important. I'm not wanted." Ideas like this release their poison into every relationship, opportunity, and circumstance throughout life.

...There are many ways and many turns of life where rejection finds its way into the human spirit. The spirit becomes the dumping ground.

...Insecurity and resentment are two other culprits that find their way into many a human spirit.[2]

We must recognize these harsh realities if we are to ever become Christlike to any extent. *All of us have those dark thought patterns*, and we can only rid ourselves of them by understanding what they are and what choices we must make to repent of them.

Corley makes further observations about the offensiveness of this "dumping ground" of hurts and dark thoughts:

Some souls live with so much rage and uncleanness pushed down into their spirits that most of their lives are controlled by devices set up to compensate for their trash. They try to cover up resentment, rejection, hatred, insecurity, guilt, etc. But, in actuality, little is covered. All of these send forth an "odor" as vile as that of a garbage dump. ...

It is difficult, if not impossible, to hide the odor of a skunk. It is [just] as difficult to hide resentment, hatred, insecurity, rejection, guilt, or lust. The same is true of a person who uses tobacco, alcohol, or other drugs. Each carries its own telltale sign.

...The saddest thing is that the techniques used to cover emotional and spiritual trash become second nature to many. The spiritual defilement never allows the one in whom it works to become genuine, especially in relationships with others. ...[3]

It should not be a shameful thing for us to have such spiritual uncleanness; such is common to man, often because of traumatic experiences in the past over which we had little or no control at the time. We must not let this knowledge cause guilt to destroy us. *But know this*: We need not have these constraining influences control us any longer! Our Lord is the God of creation; He now sits on the throne of Heaven with all power and authority. We are His precious possession.

4. Demonic Reinforcement of Dark Thinking

Satan reinforces and empowers our dark thoughts!

Do you mean that a Christian hears from satan?

Yes! Satan dwells in darkness; therefore, he can legally dwell in all of our thoughts that are apart from the life of the indwelling Christ. He feels at home with all of our thoughts that are rooted in self-seeking and self-protecting, because they are *thoughts of darkness*!

Let us not get hung up on doctrinal arguments about whether "true" Christians can or cannot be "demon possessed." If "possessed" means *ownership*, then the second chapter of the Book of Ephesians clearly proves that either Christ or satan is our slave owner; there is no "in-between" possibility. However, the word translated *possessed* means "influenced by" (the literal meaning of the Greek word *diamonizomai* in Matthew 8, Mark 5, and Luke 8). In that sense, the answer to the question is resoundingly yes, for satan uses deception to influence our thoughts. Christ warned us that satan would "...if possible, destroy the very elect..." (see Mt. 24:24; Mk. 13:22). Matthew has 'deceive', Mark has 'seduce'

The "strongholds" of satan are human patterns of thinking. Ever since his total defeat at Calvary, satan's power and authority comes only from that given to him by human will. Our thoughts of darkness give him the authority to deceive us and to reinforce our dark thoughts. As the "father of lies" and the master deceiver (see Jn. 8:44), he does it in such a way that we "naturally" believe those amplified dark thoughts are our own.

Christians are not immune to this. We were created for fellowship with God, but every aspect of our lives in which Christ is not central invites demonic influence and domination, often without our awareness or willingness. The vast majority of Spirit-led, Bible-believing Christians today actually have demonic reinforcement in *some* areas of their lives and thoughts!

It is important to realize that this does not imply *total possession* of the entire person by one or more demons of satan (although that is satan's objective in influencing us through demons). It refers to demonic *reinforcement* of certain aspects of our physical bodies and/or our thoughts and attitudes. That reinforcement manifests itself in "embedded emotional empowerments" which are hidden below the surface of cognitive awareness, beyond rational control, and driving us in powerful unChristlike ways.

In any case, we *do not have to remain* in bondage to our dark thought patterns! No demonic reinforcements of our dark thinking patterns have any right whatsoever to trespass in our hearts! The only authority any dark-reinforcing spirit can claim is the authority we give to it by our choices. Until now, we gave this permission by default, out of unawareness and ignorance. We need not tolerate it any longer. We only need to renounce the sin area associated with it, and choose to no longer tolerate it in our lives.

The road to deliverance begins and ends with the lordship of Christ Jesus over every area of demonic influence. This requires two determined decisions of those who would be free from bondage: (a) to renounce, deny, detest, and refuse the sin-pleasures at the heart of that demonic influence; and (b) to saturate their thoughts with Christ.

This often requires a determined stand on the Scriptures:

1. "Even so consider [reckon] yourselves to be dead to sin, but alive to God in Christ Jesus" (Rom. 6:11).

2. "For sin shall not be master over you, for you are not under law, but under grace" (Rom. 6:14).

3. "For no temptation has overtaken you but such is common to man; and God is faithful, who will not allow you to be tempted beyond what you are able, but with the temptation He will provide the way of escape also, that you may be able to endure it" (1 Cor. 10:13).

This requires us to renounce these sins and our desire for them, which in turn requires us to admit that we need our Lord's help. This may be extremely difficult in some cases. Some people are so deep in their bondage or so weak in their faith that they need the help of other members of the Body of Christ. Ministries of exorcism are viable and needed today to break the demonic bondages over people in these situations. This frees them long enough to become believers and to grow in their faith in Christ so they themselves can "turn on the light of Christ" unto victory. No ministry that *lacks the power of Christ Jesus* to cope with such demonic situations in people will be effective!

Exorcism is not sufficient by itself—even Christ Jesus made it clear that something good and powerful must be placed within once an evil influence has been removed (see Lk. 11:24-26). Full deliverance requires counseling plus encouragement of faith, all within the context of real, loving Christian fellowship. Christian love is the greatest and most important ingredient to wholeness. At all times, Christ must be held central in the subject's attention. Seek Christ; put Him first in thought and attitude. Desire fellowship with Him, and His grace will be sufficient for full deliverance.

5. Distancing in Interpersonal Relationships

We noted earlier that dark thought patterns result when we subconsciously adopt self-protecting or self-seeking goals to minimize pain or obtain some semblance of pleasure (even if masochistic pleasure). It follows that we will also subconsciously adopt various strategies of dealing with other people that match those self-seeking goals. Our behavior—which is based on those strategies—in turn wreaks havoc in our interpersonal relationships, our marriages, and our church fellowships.

We develop countless distancing strategies, especially in the volatile marriage relationship. Some of the most powerful ones include perfectionism, dominance, and workaholism. These distancing strategies are a common source of the contention that is so characteristic of damaged interpersonal relationships.

We seek a sense of security and significance through our personal relationships with our marriage partners, family members, friends, and fellow Christians, but we are destined to fail. No human being is capable of providing fulfillment, security, and significance to us—no matter how much that person loves us or wants to meet our needs. Our only hope for fulfillment is found in the indwelling Christ alone! That is why people inevitably disappoint us over time. Our self-nature, in turn, reacts to protect us from the pain of disappointment and rejection by erecting subtle barriers or walls (psychologists call them "defense mechanisms").

The only way to stop this inevitable disintegration of our interpersonal relationships is to *choose* to embrace the pain (i.e., to tear down our defensive walls and barriers). This allows the indwelling Christ to minister His love, acceptance, and value to us and our loved ones. That "choosing" has *two* components: *the choice to put aside personal seeking* for significance, fulfillment, self-worth, and abandoning self utterly unto Him; and *the choice to tear down every inner barrier* erected to avoid hurt inflicted by others. Christ alone is our source for love, acceptance, security, purpose and protection.

6. "Co-dependency"

Psychologists have coined a term that is widely used today for certain aspects of troubled marriage relationships: *co-dependency*. But it is a confusing and poorly understood term. It describes relationships where self-seeking strategies are so strong that they render true love impossible. One or both partners in such a relationship so intensely seek personal affirmation from the other that they are not free to constructively love the other partner. In most cases, this intense need is accompanied by aberrant behavior and thought patterns that are destructive to the relationship. These "dysfunctional" or aberrant patterns are in turn usually rooted in traumatic situations that occurred earlier in life when the person was unable to cope (some recognized, and others buried deep in the unconscious memory). One of the most common types of dysfunctional patterns (especially for women) is abysmal self-esteem rooted in victims of prolonged rejection and verbal abuse occurring in childhood in a dysfunctional family of origin.

Both partners must face head-on the seriousness and full reality of their present tragic situation in order to be healed. It may be difficult to accept, but the truth is that despite any temporary "patching up" of a relationship, the situation will not improve over time, but will actually worsen. The "yo-yo" cycles of pain, protective distancing, and extreme co-dependency will continue to intensify and increase in frequency unless the root problems are dealt with.

Healing only comes when the co-dependent partners(s) travel the painful (and incredible) route of inner heart healing. This includes: (a) discovering the root causes of the aberrant behavior and thought patterns; (b) dumping those root causes and their accompanying embedded emotional empowerments onto Christ at Calvary; and (c) personally appropriating the grace of our Lord Christ Jesus until He sovereignly satisfies the inner need for personal affirmation.

Any partner who continues to be driven by an unfulfilled need for personal affirmation will inadvertently *support and reinforce* the other spouse's aberrant behavior and thought patterns. This makes it difficult for the inner heart healing process of painful discovery and the incredible healing to take place.

This healing process involves such a drastic change in our patterns of thinking that it is *humanly* impossible! It can only occur as we willfully yield to the influence and control of the Holy Spirit of Christ Jesus indwelling. We can only yield to that *control* when certain barriers in our hearts are cut away and removed.

How? Jesus said "Whoever seeks to keep his [self-] life shall lose it, and whoever loses his [self-]life shall preserve it " (Lk. 17:33; see also Mt. 10:39; Mk. 8:35; Lk. 9:24; Jn. 12:25). That is not just a true statement of theology unto salvation in Christ. It is also a very practical application in the marriage relationship.

As a man, I have some deep emotional needs that I desperately hope my wife will fulfill in our marriage. She as a woman has some deep emotional needs that she desperately hopes I will fulfill in our marriage. Nothing is surprising about that.

However, if my mentality is need-oriented, i.e., that of trying everything I can think of to get her to meet my needs, she can't. Likewise, if her mentality is need-oriented, i.e., that of trying everything she can think of to get me to meet her needs, I can't. The result is frustration and contention, which continues to get worse as the years go by. Our inabilities to meet each other's needs under that framework of thinking are due to two reasons. First some of my needs, as well as hers, are such that only Christ indwelling is capable of meeting them. He has so created us that we need Him, and only Him, to be complete in a full sense. (These needs I classify under the heading "personal affirmation.") The second reason is, even if out of love she wants to meet my needs, she is not free to do so because she is bound by her own needs. Likewise, even if I, out of love, want to meet her needs, I am not free to do so because I am bound by my own needs.

Suppose, though, that I totally change my thinking from self/need orientation to servanthood, a change the Bible calls repentance. Suppose I now take the attitude, "Never mind my needs, Lord; only You can help me with them. But how can I meet my wife's needs? What can I do to help her, honor her, build her up, and serve her?" Consider she does likewise with me. As I try to live according to that attitude, an amazing thing begins to happen. My needs begin to be met, but in a far deeper and more satisfying way than I had ever intended—and all without my expecting it. The same happens with her needs. Why? First, the Lord meets the needs that He alone can. Second, those of my needs that were pure selfishness, the Lord takes away. But third, my wife, now beginning to become free from her needs by my attempts to truly honor and serve her, is more able to function as Christ our Creator intends her to. So I begin to become freer to serve her and her, me. This actually works, and marvelously so!

The more we try to live by *self*-seeking, the less our seekings succeed. It is only when we *stop* living by self-seeking that we become all our Lord intends us to be, namely *Christlike*. Our greatest proving ground to learn this principle is our marriage relationships!

7. The Important Issue of Human Sexuality

Human sexuality is essentially a *paradigm*—it is not essentially physiological. It is a way of thinking, a full set of personal identities, values, and a sense of purpose in life. This fact is of great importance in repentance unto inner heart healing, since our identity as persons is intrinsic to inner heart healing processes. None of us are merely "persons"—we are either male or female. We cannot escape this fact.

Just what is masculinity and femininity according to God? What are the biblical and practical paradigms of human sexuality? What does it mean to be maturely masculine or feminine? What are our social, psychological, moral, and spiritual responsibilities as men and women? We studied these issues in Chapter 3 earlier in this book. It all distills down to *love-motivated servanthood* in the specific forms unique to masculinity and femininity.

This is crucial to inner heart healing because we cannot ignore the role of God-ordained sexuality in our search for healing and deliverance. Each of us must be affirmed in our unique paradigm—as a male person or as a female person. (We are not referring to the physiological aspects of sex here, but of the deep sense of worth, value, and purpose as male and female individuals.) Our human spirits cry out for that affirmation.

The most common root of dysfunctionally-rooted reactions and behavior patterns is inadequate affirmation through non-sexual familial love and tender care. This especially concerns affirmation by the father, which should be a normal part of our maturing process through puberty and adolescence to adulthood. The absence of this paternal affirmation considerably hinders us from being Christ's channels of light, life, and love to our spouses and children.

8. "Healing of Memories"

The somewhat misleading phrase *healing of memories* is used by many authors to refer to certain critical steps in what we here call inner heart healing. This is "somewhat misleading" because the "healing" does not involve the memories *per se*, but rather centers on the shame, bondage, self-protecting strategies, and embedded emotional empowerments behind those strategies that are *linked* to the memories. Our buried memories themselves need to be first rooted out by the indwelling Holy Spirit of

Christ Jesus because of the psychological phenomenon of *denial.*

To the best of my knowledge, the phrase "healing of memories" was first coined by Agnes Sanford several decades ago. She wrote extensively about this concept:

> ...any wound to the soul [sic: human spirit] so deep that it is not healed by our own self-searching and prayers is inevitably connected with a *subconscious awareness* of sin, either our own sins or our *grievous reactions* to the sins of others. ... Therapy that heals these deep wounds could be called the *forgiveness of sins* or it could be called the *healing of memories.* Whatever one calls it, there are in many of us wounds so deep that only the meditation of *someone else* to whom we may "bare our grief" can heal us.[4]

Inner heart healing only comes when our detrimental reactions to dysfunctionally-rooted traumas and their accompanying embedded emotional empowerments are *utterly surrendered* to Christ on Calvary. With such emotionally powerful traumas, the resulting detrimental reactions (what Sanford calls "wounds so deep") almost always are deeply embedded in our subconscious and powerfully affect our feelings and behavior in the years following an original traumatic event. We must utterly surrender these reactions to Christ on Calvary.

Was Sanford a bit extreme in saying, "...only the meditation of someone else...can heal us"? All steps to this healing are acts of faith that we must make ourselves, and it is theoretically possible to do so without the help of a trusted fellow Christian. In practice, however, embedded emotional empowerments hinder our faith and our choices at the most critical times (particularly when the wounds are deep). For that reason, anyone seeking inner heart healing should have at least a prayer partner if not a counselor walk through the sometimes difficult healing process with them.

The emotional release of our embedded emotional empowerments is perhaps the most *vital* and *difficult* step in the healing process. Our dysfunctionally-rooted emotions must be replaced by the love of Christ before our healing can be completed! Sanford said it well: "What, then, is Christian love? It is a powerful, radiant and life-giving emotion, charged with healing power both to the one who learns to love and the one who is loved. To some people, this great love comes as a free gift from God, but most of us need to learn it."[5]

9. Personal Ministry Responsibilities

With so many Christians in desperate need of inner heart healing, there is an urgent need for our Lord to raise up believers who are called to help others walk through the painful but marvelous path of deep repentance unto inner heart healing. I call those brothers and sisters "personal ministries."

As we just said, the inner heart healing process usually requires that another Christian help us by walking with us through the healing steps. It should be someone to whom we make ourself personally accountable. When the Holy Spirit begins to deal with an issue involving our emotions, our personal faith is often "messed up" in peculiar ways. We often cannot exercise faith in the specific areas where our faith is lacking. There is too much distorted thinking and too many ambivalent emotions intertwined with it. This is where a compassionate and prayerful partner and/or counselor can help us take the step of faith and press through to victory and freedom.

Prayer partners and/or counselors help us in at least four important ways:

1. They help us seek the Lord and discern what specific areas of darkness in our thoughts need to be surrendered unto Him.

2. They help us surrender those areas in faith.

3. They help empower our faith in seeking and yielding to the indwelling Holy Spirit of Christ Jesus at each step.

4. They keep us from quitting prematurely or becoming diverted or misled at the most dangerous stages. (These are the points when we are feeling the long-pent-up embedded emotional empowerments behind the dysfunctionally-rooted hang-ups. These emotions must immediately be surrendered to Christ on Calvary at the very point when we are most tempted to quit.)

Christians with such personal ministries have an additional responsibility to seek the Lord for discernment. The individuals God calls in the Body of Christ through which He ministers this inner heart healing must be mature—not only in their own inner righteousness, but also in their ability to discern the true inner needs of others. They must be mature enough to freely yield to the Lord to use them to minister to those needs in love-motivated and Spirit-empowered servanthood.

The ministry of intercession is especially vital in Christian fellowships to undergird such love-motivated and Spirit-empowered discernment and servanthood.

These personal ministries of prayer-partnership intercession and/or counseling are very costly, however.

God gives us our ministries, but we must become broken to the point where we are willing to lay down "our ministry" to Him—without any expectation of Him ever giving it back to us. This willful surrender is a vital qualification for Spirit-empowered ministry.

During the 1980's, many believers who were raised up into ministry and demonstrated a powerful anointing during the "Charismatic Movement," found themselves on the "back burner" in the Kingdom of God, or on the "backside of the Midian desert." During the last decade, many of them yielded to the Lord and are now being prepared for the next move of God.

End Notes: Chapter Seven

1. Corley, Ed. "The Human Spirit—Dumping Ground of the Emotions." *Maschil*, June-July 1990, (a publication of the Berean Gospel Fellowship, Box 667, Lincolnton, GA 30817), p. 4.

2. Corley. "The Human Spirit," p. 4.

3. Corley. "The Human Spirit," p. 4.

4. Sanford, Agnes. *The Healing Gifts of the Spirit* (New York, NY: Harper & Row Publishers, 1966), pp. 126-127. Used by permission of Harper & Row Publishers.

5. Agnes Sanford, *The Healing Light* (New York, NY: Ballantine Books, 1972), p. 51. Copyright © 1947 by Macalester Park Publishing Company. Used by permission of Macalester Park Publishing Company.

PART III

Walking Through
Inner Heart Healing

We now address the deeply personal (and painful) *practical, experiential* aspects of inner heart healing. We first discuss several elements that I personally found to be essential, and several other aspects I found to be surprising (and non-intuitive). We then specifically discuss many forms of dysfunctionally-rooted and detrimental aberrations that are most common today, even among "Spirit-filled" Christian interpersonal relationships.

Chapter Eight

Essential and Non-Intuitive Aspects of Inner Heart Healing Processes

Inner heart healing is not a trivial thing; it is a *major walk in faith.* It is not a step of "basic salvation," but a significant *advancement* in our personal relationship with our Lord Christ Jesus. Inner heart healing produces deep personal peace, restores the joy of our salvation, and dramatically increases our ministry effectiveness within the Body of Christ, but *its essence is personal sanctification* through the purging of tenacious aspects of our sinnature. This purging process involves such a difficult walk of faith for most of us that it is virtually impossible to do without deep commitment to God's purpose and love in it.

I learned that lesson through personal experience. In 1991 through 1993 I walked through the process of inner heart healing three times; each dealt with different dysfunctionally-rooted self-protecting and self-seeking goals, strategies, and behavior habits. It turned out that I had three dysfunctional roots that were strong during the half dozen years before I turned 21: (a) a deep sense of personal worthlessness and lack of purpose to life; (b) social inferiority to my peers; and (c) powerful emotional shocks (career choice difficulty, male inadequacy, and love ambivalence) before I was emotionally mature enough to properly handle them.

It is not my intent to "make a doctrine out of my personal experience." Everybody's experiences with inner heart healing will be different from everyone else's. However, I here share both (a) what I found to be vital determinations/commitments on my part in order to complete the walk; and (b) some lessons I learned that I feel were highly non-intuitive.

1. Essential Commitments During the Inner Heart Healing Process

My inner heart healing process included eight specific steps of commitment on my part:

1. Commitment to the correct *purpose, goal,* and *objective.*

2. Commitment to the *required attitude of yielding to Christ.*

3. Commitment to *accountability to another Christian.*

4. Commitment to a determined and persistent *seeking of and reliance upon the indwelling Holy Spirit of Christ Jesus.*

5. Commitment to *surrender my goals/strategies to Christ.*

6. Commitment to *surrender my embedded emotions to Christ.*

7. Commitment to *release all emotional bonds to others* who were involved in the original root traumatic causes.

8. Commitment to *share my inner healing walk* with someone.

These commitments represent only a minimum set of guidelines. The point is that it is vital we "count the cost" (see Lk. 14:28). Once we choose to walk the path, we must aggressively stick to it with utter determination—no matter how painful and difficult it becomes at times. Anything less will lead to failure, and will probably reinforce and worsen our dysfunctionally-rooted behavior patterns.

Correct Purpose/Goal/Objective

The proper purpose and motive for committing to this inner heart healing process is for the indwelling Christ to have His way through us. It is not simply so we will obtain or preserve personal happiness or comfort in our relationship to Christ. In fact, the inner heart healing process involves *the very opposite of personal blessing*: deep pain and shame over our sin-nature and its removal. Perhaps the best word to express this personal experience is "bittersweet."

We must desire to become in Christ all He wants us to be. Just what does He want us to be? He wants us to become unhindered channels or vessels of His life, light, and see p. 71 love to others (especially to our spouse). He longs to flow through us to help set others free, and that requires that we become unhindered channels of Him *to ourselves first*— we cannot pass on to others what we ourselves lack.

2. Attitude of Fully Yielding to Christ

Inner heart healing is not a matter of striving for "comfortable religion"; it is an *utter abandonment* of ourselves to Christ by faith. We must take Him very seriously! Healing comes as we desperately seek His reality, holiness, and specific will for our lives. That involves our reckoning our "self," our sin-nature, crucified with Christ; and our allowing the indwelling Holy Spirit of Christ Jesus to actually effect that crucifixion.

3. Accountability to Another Christian

My own personal journey through the inner heart healing process brought the discovery that I needed another person to walk with me through the process. We usually cannot do it alone! My full release did not come solely through *my* prayers and meditations; I had to share it with at least one other brother. I could not have done it without a prayer partner—someone of the same gender, and not a member of my immediate family. This partner walked through it with me, and covered me with his intercessory prayer. He had to "discern" my human spirit's condition and what the indwelling Holy Spirit of Christ Jesus required of me next at every step.

The primary reason another Christian should help us is that when the issues we need to deal with involve our emotions, our faith is "messed up" in peculiar ways. It is very difficult for us to exercise faith in the areas where our faith is weak due to distorted thinking and ambivalent emotions. This is why the Bible exhorts fellow Christians to "bear one another's burdens..." (Gal. 6:2) and to "rejoice with those who rejoice, and weep with those who weep" (Rom. 12:15)!

4. Determined and Persistent Seeking of and Reliance Upon the Indwelling Holy Spirit

Inner heart healing is the inward working of the indwelling Holy Spirit of Christ Jesus (to the extent that we allow Him to work). We must have the attitude to seek that inner working with determination, sometimes with the intensity of desperation—always relying on Him to do the actual doing.

The Holy Spirit works tirelessly to bring total healing to us in three significant ways:

1. He reveals to our consciousness anything that hinders the flow of our Lord's light, life, and love into us and through us to others.

2. He reveals to our consciousness the underlying self-seeking and self-protecting goals, strategies, and resulting habits that cause us to effect those hindrances (albeit subconsciously most of the time).

3. He reveals to our consciousness the key traumatic events or other root causes for our adoption of those self-seeking and self-protecting goals and strategies.

5. Surrender Your Self-Protecting/Seeking Goals/Strategies to Christ

The commitment of surrender basically requires the discipline of repentance. The key to deliverance is a determined choice to no longer allow our ungodly goals and strategies to drive our thoughts and behavior. We achieve this repentance by *surrendering* them to Christ, who died on the cross to free us from them. Faith on our part is very much a part of this process, but even though we may choose to do right, He must do the enabling. This step (and the one that follows) inevitably involves intense psychological or emotional pain; that is why a commitment to "embrace that pain" is part of the process.

6. Surrender the Embedded Emotional Empowerments to Christ

The surrender of embedded emotional empowerments is perhaps the most difficult and most painful of the entire inner heart healing process. It literally requires us to actually feel, express, and vent those volatile emotions before we can release them. It required total involvement on my part—involvement of every part of my being, with every ounce of strength—to surrender these emotions to Christ.

This painful process actually works. As we obediently follow the Lord through the "fire of cleansing," He indeed removes the power of those underlying embedded emotional empowerments (and any demonic amplifications of them). However, *this is the only way* the power of those emotions can be broken and removed. Only when this has happened can these emotions be fully released to Christ. Otherwise, we will quickly revert to the original, uncrucified state of strong dysfunctionally-rooted hindrances to His flow into and through us.

7. Release All Emotional Bonds to Others Who Were Involved in the Original Root Traumatic Causes

Once the power of those underlying emotions is broken and/or removed, then (and only then) the final two steps of the inner heart healing process will be possible. Most of us have been hurt or wounded by others in life, and our attitudes toward those individuals who were involved in our root causal traumas are crucial for complete healing. Most of us with deep hurts carry painful memories of the people who deeply abused us, disappointed us, or otherwise hurt us. The hurt and pain of these traumas actually drove us to our self-protecting goals and strategies in the first place. In some cases, we may also know people who were the opposite: They were sources of great pleasure that *amplified our self-seeking strategies.* In either case, we must become emotionally neutral or "de-coupled" from them to be fully free ourselves.

This step to wholeness is therefore to forgive the people who hurt us. This is not forgiveness "unto their salvation"—only Christ can provide that. We must do this "forgiving" not for their sakes, but for *ours,* if we want final release. This forgiveness releases us from our emotional bondage to the dysfunctional sources of our self-protection. Only when we have been emotionally "de-coupled" from them will we be free to be love-motivated and Spirit-empowered servants of Christ to others! As with each of the other steps of faith in the inner heart healing process, *we* must *choose* to do the forgiving, all the while depending upon the indwelling Holy Spirit of Christ Jesus to enable the actual forgiving. It really works!

For those who were sources of pleasure, this emotional de-coupling involves applying the final stages of the *grieving process*[1] to them. Why? The original person in our memory no longer exists! This may appear to be a subtle issue, but it is important nevertheless. We are dealing with an emotional "de-coupling" from our *embedded perceptions* of a person from the past, not the actual, physical, and historical person. No matter how strong or lengthy our "history" was with the person, we need to seek emotional de-coupling from our mental concept of the person that has been embedded in us over time.

8. **Share Your Inner Healing Walk With Someone**

Final release comes when our journey is shared with someone else. We know both experientially and biblically that this is necessary for final release. We must share the story with someone else—whether it is our prayer partner, our counselor, or whoever. I also found it very therapeutic to write out a journal or diary of my experiences and progress. Whoever we choose, it must be someone we know we can trust to still accept us after learning about our dark secrets and our journey to freedom.

Sharing and confessing private matters to another person is a difficult and fearful step for any of us—especially as long as *our sense of acceptance* depends on what we think others might think about us. For this reason, we have to have such a closeness with our Lord Christ Jesus that our sense of acceptance and personal worth is dependent upon Him and only upon Him. Only when this assurance is firmly in place can we make this final step for total healing.

Virtually everyone who has been healed inwardly in these ways has experienced tremendous final release when they honestly shared their "testimony" of pain and freedom with another. This last step requires us to be honest; the human heart is so self-deceptive. This transparent honesty also helps assure us that no other important detail required for the inner heart healing has been ignored. It ensures humility—we cannot share the darker aspects of our sin-nature with someone else without being humble.

This truth is echoed in James 5:16: "Therefore, confess your sins to one another, and pray for one another, so that you may be healed. The effective prayer of a righteous man can accomplish much." James wasn't telling us we should confess our sins and failures to a priest to receive absolution of sins (only Christ can forgive sins). This Scripture concerns healing, not basic salvation. God has ordained that we find release and inner heart healing through confession to other members of the Body of Christ who love us, and through humble submission one to another!

2. What These Eight Commitments Are Not

We also should examine exactly what these eight guidelines *are not.*

First of all, these eight steps of commitment are not a *program to be followed,* either as a self-exercise or in group therapy. I don't want to ever hear or read about "Sherrerd's Eight Steps for Inner Heart Healing"!

These things require determined and aggressive initiatives on our part, but inner heart healing cannot be accomplished solely by self-effort. These things are not something we choose to *do;* they are things we choose to *yield* to the indwelling Holy Spirit of Christ Jesus working in us. The actual doing is His, not ours. These are steps of crucifixion of self, and self cannot crucify self. As long as self is doing the work, then its very actions prove that it is clinging to its life and not being crucified. Only Christ can do it.

Group therapy is not sufficient for full inner heart healing either, even though this can often be of great value in the Body of Christ. Efforts to bring about inner heart healing in most deep, dysfunctionally-rooted behavior deviations by group therapy can be compared to trying to cure pneumonia with cough medicine. Even the manual of a leading multi-step treatment program (of which steps 4 through 7 roughly correspond to this concept of inner heart healing process) recognizes these limitations with these words:

NOTICE This book is designed to provide information regarding the subject matter covered. It is provided with the understanding that the publisher and author are not engaged in rendering individualized professional services. These processes and questions are intended for group or individual study, and [are] not designed to be a substitute for one-to-one professional therapy when such help is necessary.[2]

This inner heart healing process is *not a psychological exercise*. Again, it is the inward working of the indwelling Holy Spirit of Christ Jesus. He alone leads us through each step and enables all results. Some knowledge of human psychology is helpful, particularly when we are helping others through counseling to walk the path. However, it is first, last, and always a *spiritual ministry* that goes far beyond human understanding or ability.

Just what does our Lord do and not do? Many of us have been taught that if we simply pray that the Lord do something, if we have enough "faith," He will do "it." The Lord doesn't actually "do" anything *per se*. He *becomes!*

1. *He becomes our readily available source of life*—the fulfillment of our real, deep needs (of acceptance and fulfillment). This is what the Bible means by Christ being our "Tree of Life." It is our very lack of acceptance and fulfillment (rejection and emptiness) that led to our dysfunctionally-rooted self-seeking and self-protecting goals and strategies in the first place! These goals and strategies dominate our behavior in non-Christian ways. Once He becomes our actual Source, we no

longer need those goals and strategies to protect us from pain nor to bring us the pleasures we desire.

Before He can become that source in our personal lives, we must walk through these aspects of repentance:

a. From our "natural" aversion against God.

b. From our intrinsic sin of unbelief of His ability to protect and provide for us.

c. From the specific self-protecting goals and strategies, after His indwelling Holy Spirit reveals it/them to us.

2. *He becomes our scapegoat for the dysfunctionally-rooted emotional empowerment* that "forced" us to behave in the self-protecting and self-seeking ways. The ability of Christ Jesus to actually take the empowerment away is such a miraculous thing that I had to *personally experience it* before I had sufficient faith in it to teach and encourage others to seek it.

3. Those Aspects Which I Found to Be Particularly Surprising

I discovered many aspects of the process of inner heart healing that truly surprised me.

First, **denial.** I was surprised to discover the *reality* of the psychological principle of *denial.* Embedded deep in our created nature is a natural bodily reaction that responds to sustained high emotional stress with a local form of amnesia. It efficiently "de-couples" our emotional stresses from our memory of the events that originally triggered them. I experienced four highly emotional shocks between the ages of 18 and 21 which I was totally unprepared to handle at the time. When the Lord finally enabled me to remember them during the inner heart healing process, I was shocked to realize that *I had been so totally oblivious of them more than 40 years*! At first I couldn't comprehend how these particularly vivid events in my life could ever be forgotten. But these things were so thoroughly forgotten and buried that only the inner workings of the indwelling Holy Spirit of Christ Jesus could bring them to my conscious memory.

God, in His wisdom, created us this way so we could physiologically survive traumatic events. The human body cannot sustain intense "emoting" day in and day out for any significant length of time. This level of stress creates an unbalance in key body hormones such as adrenaline, estrogen, etc., that, if sustained, would lead to a major physical breakdown, and possibly death if sustained long enough. So without the phenomenon of "denial," any major traumatic event triggering emotional shock would kill us in time.

Second, the **impact of embedded emotions.** I was surprised to see how those traumatic events early in my life (both the actual memories and the original emotions, in their original intensity) remained intact within me for those four decades. This happened even though this "denial" kept the events from my consciousness. They also dominated my behavior in ways totally beyond my awareness.

Those dormant but powerful dysfunctionally-rooted memories detrimentally impacted my entire life by preventing or at least hindering my being what God primarily intended me to be. He wants us all to be yielded vessels of His light, life, and love to others, particularly to loved ones and others close to us. Despite my intense intentions (my *obsession*) to be the best husband, father, and Christian I could be, it was impossible for me to come even close to what could be reasonably expected of a redeemed sinner!

It is vitally important for each of us to seek inner heart healing, and to submit to the pain of it for the sake of our loved ones and for the sake of others in the Body of Christ—not for our own personal happiness or well-being.

Third, the **role of ambivalence.** I was also surprised to discover the powerful role that *ambivalence* plays in the detrimental impacts of traumatic events. I've defined[3] this role in what I call "Sherrerd's Law of Ambivalence":

> When two or more conflicting emotions pertain to the same behavioral issue, the emotion with the most phobic [i.e., fear-related] content determines the behavioral outcome, external forces notwithstanding.

This "law" is simply one application of the truth that *pain-avoidance is a far stronger human motivation than pleasure-seeking.* It is also based upon Second Timothy 1:7, which tells us that fear is a spirit, and that it does not come from God! Unless the spirit of fear is withstood by the Holy Spirit of Christ Jesus in us, it will dominate us with its great power. My personal experience verified that this law of ambivalence was virtually dominant. I am simply amazed in hindsight that even mild and irrational fears won out over intensely powerful love and clearly righteous rationality. Nevertheless, this happened over and over again throughout my life!

Inner heart healing cannot possibly occur without going through the pain of having these things brought to our consciousness, since the root causes of our dysfunctionally-rooted failings are so embedded in us. Once we are able to recognize them for what they are, we can surrender them to our Lord Christ Jesus! There is no other way!

Demonic exorcism is not sufficient, although demonic forces may well be involved! Yes, they seek out the darkness in our thought patterns that are not submitted to the lordship of our Lord Christ Jesus, and then *amplify* it. But they are not the *cause* of our dysfunctionally-rooted aberrations—the darkness is! The root darknesses must be removed so that inner heart healing can occur, or else the dysfunctionally-rooted aberrations will continue.

Even a powerful "visitation" of the Holy Spirit during an altar call isn't sufficient! I believe we should not simply encourage people to come forward to the altar for *inner heart healing prayer*; much more is required! Only the inner working of the indwelling Holy spirit of Christ Jesus can root out and remove the darkness, and that takes much time—it requires *deep repentance* on our part.

 Fourth, the **depth of our forgiveness by Chirst.** This totally involved surrender of our darkness to Christ centers around three basic sins we've mentioned before: (a) our intrinsic aversion against God; (b) our doubts that Christ is within us and that He is really sufficient for our protection and fulfillment; and (c) the specific self-protecting strategies, the specific dysfunctionally-rooted darknesses that lie at the root of our impedance to the flow of Christ's love to and through us.

One reason for my intrinsic aversion against God was my failure to fully appreciate Christ's forgiveness of my sins through His sacrifice on Calvary. At the time of my original conversion, the only "sin" I could remember and repent of was my theft of a penny from my sixth-grade teacher. For more than 20 years, I had only a "penny's worth" of appreciation of Christ's forgiveness of sin.

When the depth of dysfunctionally-rooted sins were revealed to me, it was a very difficult step of faith for me to expect Him to forgive me for inflicting pain on another person who was very dear to me at the time, and to remove the tremendous guilt and remorse I now realized had accompanied this sin. But in my case, it was easy for me to yield to Christ the mental aspects of my darknesses. I thought that the very idea events that occurred some 40 years ago could still control or even influence my life today was utterly ludicrous. Once that absurdity came to my attention, I, of course, yielded it to Jesus.

Fifth, the **miraculous release of our embedded emotional empowerments.** The emotional content of the dysfunctionally-rooted darknesses in my life, however, was totally different. I was quite surprised at the "crazy" process I had to follow to dump them onto Christ and be set free. I had to allow myself to fully feel, express, and vent those emotions again, in their original intensity! That was painful! I had to feel them *in the presence of Christ on Calvary*, in conscious awareness of Christ and His love and anxiousness to remove them from me. I could not have surrendered those emotional empowerments to Him without again feeling and expressing them.

I experienced painful brokenness in this inner heart healing process, but it was worth it! The pain was short-lived and it came near the final step in release and deliverance. Then I was able to actually feel the joy of my salvation, and to truly know the peace and joy of Christ after all those years! Even more practical, in my case, I was actually able to feel and express my deep love for my wife, my family, and for others in the Body of Christ! Christ is indeed more than sufficient.

End Notes: Chapter Eight

1. We discuss the grieving process later in Chapter Eleven.

2. *Friends in Recovery, The Twelve Steps—A Spiritual Journey*, Recovery Publications, Inc., 1988), pg. xv. This work has been revised and is now available as *The Twelve Steps for Christians* (San Diego, CA: RPI Publishing, Inc., 1994), ISBN 0-941405-57-5, (pbk).

3. I'll say "I" Until someone points out to me one who really deserves the "credit" for first articulating it.

Chapter Nine

Root Needs, Voids, Hurts, and Dysfunctionally-Rooted Responses

Dysfunctionally-rooted hindrances to our interpersonal relationships plague the *vast majority* of us. A large number of adults (even "Spirit-filled" Christians) carry deep traumatic burdens in their lives and relationships.

1. 96 Percent of Us

Jim Conway provides an incredible statistic about how universal this problem is. He studied the problems of the adult children of alcoholic parents, and quoted Ann Goetting[1], Mavis Hetherintong[2] and Cynthia Longfellow,[3] who have conducted and analyzed research about these dysfunctionally-rooted problems:

> ...two of the major writers for children of alcoholics say the problem is really much greater:... "Children of alcoholics are but the visible tip of a much larger social iceberg which casts an invisible shadow

over as much as *96 percent of the population* in this country. They are the children of trauma."... (They are referring to all children from emotionally or legally divorced homes or dysfunctional families.)

Surviving their childhoods rather than experiencing them, these children of trauma have also had to surrender a part of themselves very early in life. Not knowing what hit them, and suffering a sourceless sense of pain in adulthood, they perpetuate the denial and minimization which encased them in dysfunctional roles, rules, and behaviors.

These writers go on to point out that the "children of trauma" generally come from perfectionistic, judgmental, critical, or non-loving families who appear normal and function well on the surface. In all of these families rigidity [and inconsistency] prevents normal childhood development. In the name of love, children are ignored, isolated, abandoned, and abused.[4]

Ninety-six percent! This is not just referring to some group of poor unfortunate souls "over there" who need our prayers. It is virtually all of us! It is you and me!

The syndrome described in the phrase, "the denial and minimization which encased them in dysfunctional roles, rules, and behaviors" has also been called by some authors "grievous responses to dysfunctional traumas." Throughout this book, these are designated as "self-seeking and self-protecting goals, strategies, and behaviors." It is extremely common for these defense mechanisms to give rise to interpersonal distancing barriers.

I personally doubt if any of us are totally free of them. Our individual situations differ only in their specific traumatic causes and degree of severity. For some of us, these barriers are so mild that a simple repentance on our part will bring release and freedom. However, in a significant number of us (including "Spirit-filled" Christians), dysfunctional influences in our pasts have been so traumatic and overwhelming during particularly vulnerable periods, that the hang-ups they created are too strong to yield in *simple* repentance. They require the full gamut of deep surrender form of repentance inherent in the inner heart healing process.

We all have three intrinsic needs: (a) to know we are to serve, (b) to serve, and (c) to have our servanthood received. These needs are powerful long-term motivations of our lives. Due to the Fall, we choose to serve "self" rather than others, and those needs have become horribly distorted. Our need to be a servant has been transformed into a need for identity and value. Our need to serve has become a need for purpose and fulfillment. Our need to have our servanthood received has been transformed into a driving need to be accepted, loved, and respected *by other persons.*

We now depend on the cooperation of others for our fulfillment instead of having our needs automatically satisfied by God's design. The problem with this man-centered system is that those "others" won't "cooperate" because they are so wrapped up in *their own self-seeking* and self-protecting that they can't. When those "others" inevitably disappoint us, these powerful long-term motivations remain unsatisfied, and that disappointment often appears to be life-threatening. That gives rise to fear that intensifies our self-seeking and self-protecting efforts with an element of bondage. The vicious cycle grows and accelerates, as does the deterioration and destruction of relationships.

Our marriages suffer the most tragic consequences. Instituted by God to provide rich companionship, support, and encouragement, this relationship was never meant to be our primary source of acceptance and fulfillment. This can only come from our personal relationship with our Lord Christ Jesus. Nevertheless, we demand these things from our spouses, and we begin a dysfunctionally-rooted downward spiral that will destroy our marriages and relationships if we fail to turn to God.

The most vital and misunderstood issue of the marriage relationship, and *the most basic root cause of dissatisfaction* among wives and husbands alike, may be described by "Sherrerd's Law of Marital Ineptitude":

God has created us male and female, and He created us so that no husband or wife (no matter how "ideal" he/she may appear to be) is capable of providing the spouse's deepest need: a sense of being fully loved and accepted unconditionally; a deeply settled awareness of their intrinsic worth, purpose, and identity; with a healthy and full acceptance of their "self" and sexuality.

When we fail to receive acceptance and value from others, we experience *rejection* and *emptiness*. Since pain-avoidance is a more powerful human motivation than pleasure-seeking, we react to our void in dysfunctionally-rooted ways. We develop self-seeking and self-protecting goals and strategies of all sorts, and most of them involve building "distancing barriers" between us and any possible "threat." (Unfortunately, the closest "threat" is usually our spouse!) When this is coupled with an intense drive to find acceptance in fulfillment by *our own efforts*, then our self-seeking and self-protecting drives virtually control all we do and say to others—in marriage, on the job, and even in our Christian ministries. This goes on for life, unless we surrender them to Christ on Calvary in inner heart healing.

Many of us suffer from more than simple rejection and emptiness. Many of us deal with a complex mixture of traumatic events marked by a highly emotional set of phobic and self-abnegating aspects, from experiences in early life before we were mature enough to rationally handle them. Many of our problems stem from efforts to protect ourselves from such dysfunctional situations during childhood. These traumatic events can terribly distort and amplify our self-seeking and self-protecting goals and strategies.

For example, many adults not only suffer from the usual forms of rejection and emptiness—they also have to deal with the trauma created by divorced parents or an absent father; or strong verbal or physical abuse by a parent; or the scars of sexual abuse; or battle fatigue in war. Many suffer because they were not adequately affirmed as the male or female person God intended them to be. Dysfunctionally-rooted amplifications of these "core voids," and the behavior patterns rooted in them, can be astonishingly brutal.

"Self-seeking" and "self-protecting" goals, strategies, and behavior patterns can be avoided or eliminated by allowing Christ to be our only Tree of Life. We don't have to distinguish between self-seeking and self-protecting in the inner heart healing process. *We simply deal with whatever the indwelling Holy Spirit of Christ Jesus uproots.* Although there is nothing shameful about being caught up in this self-seeking and self-protecting syndrome, it is shameful to cling to them in face of so great a salvation and deliverance in Christ.

2. Rejection

Some of the most common causes of distancing for self-protection are "battle wounds from rejection." These "inner wounds" are the inevitable result of traumatic experiences of rejection (i.e., by one or both parents, spouses, or other people close to us) when we are weak in Christian faith or have none at all. We fall into this paradigm quite "innocently" by reacting to situations usually beyond our control at the time, having no guidelines for proper reaction or emotional management of the situations.

It is estimated that about 40 percent of all adult Americans are distressed to some extent by this rejection. More than 12 percent of all adult Americans, and more than 25 percent of American marriages, are *severely* distressed by it. According to Frank and Ida Hammond, *schizophrenia*, (a psychotic condition marked by loss of contact with reality, and by a disintegration of personality with disordered feelings, thought patterns, and behavior), as caused by severe dysfunctionally-rooted rejection, characterizes "about one out of eight persons."[5] This is often the case in our modern "Western" society, where personal ambitions take precedence over truly loving and caring for our families.

These deep hurts can nearly always be traced to a person being unwanted, unloved, and rejected by others *at times when the person was unable to cope with it,* often in early childhood (or even in the womb). When Christ indwelling is far from being our "rock" of love-security, the pain of rejection is extremely intense. Our resulting self-protecting goals and strategies to mitigate that pain, may take the form of obsessive jealously, workaholism, legalistic perfectionism, or various addictions. They are usually buried or hidden in our sub-consciousness, but they remain powerful forces in our lives that reinforce irrational behavior patterns destructive to us and others in our interpersonal relationships.

The "battle wounds" from these traumatic rejection experiences lead to self-protecting goals with a unique two-part pattern: (a) a desire to *protect* self from being hurt from further rejection; and (b) a desire to somehow *find* a sense of love-security. Since these two goals conflict, they lead to two conflicting strategies: (a) to *distance* oneself from other people who are emotionally close (i.e., parents, children, spouse, friends), often through extreme behavior patterns of anger, hostility, aggressiveness, etc.; and yet also (b) to *demand love-security* from those very people!

According to Hammond, this inner warring in turn gives rise to two warring "families" of self-protecting behavior patterns and thoughts of darkness (they refer to them as groups of demons): (a) darkness-abiding drives of *outward hostility* against others; and (b) darkness-abiding drives of *inward rejection* against one's self.[6] By *darkness* we mean any thought pattern in us that has not (yet) been submitted to the lordship of Christ Jesus.

Demonic forces seek out this darkness and, once they find it, they amplify its intensities. All of our "dark" thinking patterns (i.e., those not yielded to the indwelling Christ) are open targets for reinforcement by satan and his demonic forces. This is done in such a deceptive way that a person may believe that these thoughts are their own, and represent "the way life is." This is especially true with "dark" thought patterns resulting from traumatic perceived rejection.

"Darkness-abiding drives of outward rebellion" include suspicions, accusation of others, possessiveness, resentment, jealousy, stubbornness, unforgiveness, aggression, and bitterness. "Darkness-abiding drives of inward rejection" are strongly masochistic in nature. They include depression, suicidal tendencies, withdrawal, loneliness, phobias of various kinds, paranoia, fantasy, perfectionism, and extreme talkativeness. Darkness-abiding drives of outward rebellion *keep the true personality from seeking help*, either from God or from fellow Christians. Darkness-abiding drives of inward rejection *keep the true personality from giving and receiving love* to and from others, including God's love.

This instability is almost inevitable in home environments characterized by *distancing* between the mother and father. It is also typical of dysfunctional home environments characterized by alcoholic parent(s), emotional if not legal divorce, verbal or physical abuse, or "latch-key" and "child-care" situations where both parents are absent due to work or life style. Adopted children also have a specific tendency toward it. The cause is *perceived* rejection through disapproval, if not by *actual* rejection. Victory comes only by seeking fulfillment, security, and significance from the indwelling Christ, and not by our own efforts.

3. Emptiness and Non-Identity

Our independent (self-seeking) efforts to find well-being, value, and purpose, and our defensive (self-protecting) strategies to guard us from the lack of these things (non-identity and emptiness), are closely related to our efforts to protect ourselves from rejection. All of these drives are extremely powerful. The three most common and powerful drives are *hiding, obsession,* and *sexual perversion.*

Hiding refers to all the ways we try to cover up our sense of worthlessness and inadequacy. We all do this to some extent; to be "human" requires that we have some lack of self-confidence and sense of personal value. Nevertheless, it is extremely embarrassing to have our perceived inadequacy *exposed* to others. Our efforts to cover or *hide* our shortcomings or fears are also forms of self-protection against *rejection*, since we fear that others will reject us if they ever know our inner weaknesses. However, we list these dysfunctionally-rooted reactions here since they stem from a sense of lack of identity and emptiness.

Obsessions are even more powerful dysfunctionally-rooted reactions to lack of personal identity and emptiness! They may take the form of extreme possessiveness (of things or people), or of an intense drive to perform. Possessiveness stems from our hope to find a sense of personal identity by attachment to the thing or person. When the object of our possessiveness is another person, it is extremely destructive to him or her (i.e., our spouse, child, co-dependent companion, etc.).

Another example of this drive is the obsession to obtain and exercise power to command and manipulate other people in business, politics, and the home. It is a form of idolatry, with a powerful force of bondage. Also, the drive to perform stems from our attempts to obtain a sense of value, purpose, and worthwhileness *through our own efforts*. Perfectionism and workaholism in its various forms are the most common examples. Most forms of substance abuse are also dysfunctionally rooted in this.

It is a shocking fact that the vast majority of the Christian *ministry* efforts are actually motivated by obsessions rooted in self-seeking for fulfillment and identity! Countless ministers have buried themselves in "ministry" efforts, to "feed their obsessions" to find fulfillment in their own works of the flesh, never realizing that God wants to "do the work" through them instead of them doing the work for Him.

4. Crises in Masculinity and Femininity

Sexual perversions are other very destructive dys-functionally-rooted reactions of self-efforts to find a sense of identity, significance, and acceptance.

Why? Our sense of identity and personhood is totally and intimately entwined with our sexuality. After more than 40 years under the influence of the *Playboy* men-tality, our culture has so corrupted our concepts of sexuality that even Christians regard with skepticism the biblical concept of "human sexuality as unique forms of servanthood." God's intended purpose for human sexuality (love-motivated servanthood) has been de-graded to simple measures of physical prowess in ways that dehumanize women and emasculate men.

Inadequate affirmation in childhood is by far the most common root of our dysfunctionally-rooted reactions and behavior patterns. Affirmation through non-sexual fam-ilial love and tender care, especially by the *father*, should be a normal part of our maturing process, from birth through puberty and adolescence unto adulthood.

More specifically, sexual perversion is nearly always rooted in persons who, during childhood and adolescence, are prevented for some reason from maturing in their proper sexuality paradigm (as male or female). This paradigm is essential if we are to have any sense of iden-tity and value, since we cannot separate our personhood from our gender. Our Creator equipped us to exercise the specific forms of servanthood related to our sexuality paradigm. When our unique physiological and emotional faculties, drives, and longings are not directed properly, their release becomes quite deviant.

Compulsive masturbation is the most common devian-cy of this type. Homosexualism and lesbianism are other forms that are now rapidly increasing in frequency. Pornography and sexual perversions of a criminal nature are very close cousins of this deviancy, in its most socially destructive forms.

I highly recommend two books by Leanne Payne, *Crisis in Masculinity*[7] and *The Broken Image*[8] on the subject of homosexuality and lesbianism. Payne cites several examples of successful deliverances through her counseling ministry. She not only emphasizes the dysfunctional roots for such behavior, but also makes a very interesting point: Homosexual longings, with or without specific acts, are a form of "cannibalism." Payne notes that clients attempt by close association with someone of the same gender to "acquire" some sexually-related attribute or attributes that they sense to be lacking in themselves.

Payne also points out that normally a person is affirmed as a masculine or feminine person during adolescence *by the father*. (Dalbey[9] and Wright[10] also strongly emphasize this point.) *The father*, as head of the family, nurtures both his sons and his daughters in normal familial (non-sexual) love, physical contact, and encouragement to become all they intrinsically are.

This is an extremely important observation! Homosexuality and lesbianism are rooted in the failure of a father to provide that affirmation, and in his abdication of his responsibilities to a dominant wife, either because of his absence or because of his own dysfunctionally-rooted distortions. The political claims of "gay rightists" that homosexuality is genetic and hence hopeless, is pure nonsense!

My own personal observations seem to confirm that the root dysfunctional cause of homosexualism is a lack of affirmation of the person as a masculine/feminine person during adolescence. Male homosexuality has been foreign to my direct personal experience. However, had I not have been affirmed by someone who believed in me in my early twenties, when I suffered certain emotional shocks, it is highly likely that I could have gone that route, given the near-total self-abnegations as a man that I felt at the time! Also, in two cases of lesbianism with which I am familiar, the root causes were clear. Neither woman had been affirmed as a feminine person during adolescence. One received strong parental pressure to act as a son, and the other suffered the death of her mother, which was associated with dysfunctional family circumstances of her father when she was still at an early age.

The prevailing destructive sexual/spiritual influences of "soft" pornography are carefully documented in a recent book by Dr. Judith A. Reisman, *Sort Porn Plays Hardball—Its Tragic Effects On Women, Children, & The Family*.[11] Dr. Reisman shows how the introduction of *Playboy* and other "soft"[12] pornographic magazines to the American scene since late 1953 has destroyed our culture. This paradigm totally denigrates and dehumanizes women and emasculates men, and it has been the singly most destructive force against the family in all of history.

The thrust of this cultural disintegration is the distortion of human sexuality paradigms from a God-ordained foundation in loving servanthood to selfish pleasure-seeking. This brutally distorts our affirmation as men or women from our development as mutual servants to that of mere animals who satisfy base appetites with mere "physical sexual prowess." The *Playboy* influence has tremendously amplified this deviancy. Specifically, the *Playboy* mentality, increasingly pervasive in our culture since the mid-1950s, teaches in essence:

Sex is for self-gratification; that's what women are for; anything goes, there are no absolute moral values; and men are to be aggressive.

This is, of course, a fiendish lie of satan. It is totally dehumanizing to women. But ironically, men are its worst victims! Virtually every American (and European) male of the "baby boomer" and subsequent generations has been totally bombarded with this lie since birth through every form of media, and in every aspect of our culture. We estimate that as many as eight out of every ten husbands (even Christian husbands) in this country have become so deeply brainwashed that they know nothing else!

The fact is that this lie goes against the grain of every male's "natural inclinations." He has been created for love-motivated servanthood according to Ephesians 5:22-25 and First Peter 3:7, so every fiber of his being has a "natural" propensity for loving his wife through servanthood.

So men are torn between two forces: all they've been taught, and their "natural" propensities. This triggers a civil war of major proportions that wages in their hearts, deep in the 90 percent of the "iceberg" beneath the surface of their cognitive awareness. Most of the time, all they sense is a vague but persistent uneasiness. But that war is real, and they can't handle that warfare for long; the result is that sooner or later they "take sides" with one and block out the other. If they are not in Christ, or are unaware of the biblical teachings, they will block out their natural propensity for godly love. Is it any wonder, then, that we are seeing an explosion of sexual perversion today?

Now consider the husband who *genuinely* becomes a Christian. He reads Ephesians 5 and First Peter 3, and understands and agrees with them. He actually rejoices that at last he's found truth that aligns with his natural propensities, at least to the extent he is aware of them. He genuinely and deeply loves his wife, but *he doesn't know how to express that love!* He is left with a deep, dark secret that terrifies him—he fears that if his wife ever discovers his masculine inadequacies, she will reject or ridicule him. That secret fear drives him to never allow her to come close enough to ever discover his secret weakness. (This is a gross oversimplification, but it captures the essence and the core issues. Again, it's buried below the surface of cognitive awareness, so he's unaware of how deeply his distancing hurts his wife.)

What is that deep, dark secret? If he could express it, it would go something like this:

> I want in every way to love you, my wife, as Christ loves His Church. But I know deep inside that I can't! I'm not able to! I don't know how! Something in me is blocking me! I'm only half a man! If I ever lose your respect for me as a man, I am nothing! If I'm not a man, what am I? I'm not a woman, and God didn't make any "its." That truth is too painful for me to bear. So don't you ever dare get close enough to me to find out that I'm only half a man!

This fearful husband rapidly distances himself from his wife, perhaps with moody withdrawal, workaholism, anger, violence, abuse, addictions, or countless other fruits of fear.

Why is he "only half a man"? Now that he is a genuine Christian, he is blocking out all he's been taught, and taking sides with his "natural" propensities for godly love. With the mass of satan's fiendish lie cut away, he has a gigantic void in his soul. He feels deeply emasculated. He has to yield to Jesus his High Priest to cut away all those old, erroneous habits, and replace them with biblically righteous habits of thinking and feeling. But that takes time, much time. His *inner heart healing* is a mandatory but also major undertaking.

With the help of another Christian man (a prayer partner or counselor), he can get the tumerous mass of satan's fiendish lie cut away. But that's not quite the end of it. He also needs his wife's help to learn how to love her as Christ loves (Eph. 5:25). That may seem unfair, since his wife has probably suffered due to her husband's dysfunctionally-rooted problems—but she needs to help him overcome. Their marriage is worth it.

This man's wife most probably also needs inner heart healing herself. Perhaps she has developed damaging self-seeking and self-protecting goals and strategies such as obsessive possessiveness and jealousy, legalistic perfectionism, religious addiction, mild forms of schizophrenia, etc. She needs her husband's help (especially love, compassion, understanding, and patience) as she walks through her inner heart healing process. That may seem unfair to him, since he has probably suffered due to his wife's dysfunctionally-rooted problems; but he needs to help her overcome. He also knows their marriage is worth it.

5. The Dysfunctional Downward Spiral of Even Christian Marriages

How our dysfunctionally-rooted reactions to emptiness and rejection affect Christian marriage relationships is a *major* problem. The marriages of believers are not immune to the destructive influences of these reactions.

"Sherrerd's Law of the Dysfunctional Downward Spiral of the Marriage Relationship" states:

Unless repented of through inner heart healing, the dysfunctionally-rooted self-seeking and self-protecting strategies in one or both spouses *will tend to drive the marriage relationship toward emotional if not legal divorce* through distancing over time, external influences notwithstanding.

What does a wife really need the most from her husband? What does a husband desire the most from his wife? God established the thought patterns or paradigms of masculinity and femininity long ago, and He rooted them in genuine love-motivated servanthood. After man's fall in the garden of Eden, we confused and distorted God's paradigm in our own minds through our own rebellion, sin and "self-reliance." Nevertheless, the most profound and behavior-driving needs *are not those of the flesh* (which, though intense, are short-term), but of the human *spirit*.

The most important need for any of us—regardless of gender or position—is the need for *affirmation*. Every wife needs her husband to *fully accept her as the person she is* and genuinely appreciate her as an intrinsically precious and worthy person. This acceptance and affirmation must be given *regardless of what he receives* from her, and he should consistently express those attitudes by spending enough time with her as a compassionate friend to prove that she is a priority in his life. She needs this far more than even the economic and physical security of the home!

What do wives detest the most in their marriage relationships? Wives despise the sense of *being used* by their husbands for their selfish desires.

Contrary to popular opinion and secular propaganda, husbands really need something from their wives that is far more important and hard to find than sex and good cooking: They want their wives to *respect* them. Every husband has a deep inner need for his wife to *respect him for the person he is*. This includes encouraging him in what he is striving to be and do as head of the family (in the sense of providing and caring as a loving servant). Wives should consistently express those attitudes by warmly receiving their husbands' service to them.

What do husbands detest most in their marriage relationships? Husbands despise *their wives' rejection of their service* to them. They detest their wives' insinuations or outright statements that they do not think their husbands are capable of meeting their responsibilities properly without *their intervention.*

Most marriages usually begin on the right basis. When a man and a woman make their marriage vows to each other, most of the partners genuinely intend to carry them out at the time—their love for each other drives them to make a permanent commitment. However, they also come to the altar *with deeply ingrained self-seeking and self-protecting strategies*. This led me to formulate "Sherrerd's Law of Nuptial Self-Deceit":

> No matter how genuinely we make our marriage vows, the vast majority of us enter into marriage for *self-seeking* fulfillment of our *need for identity* and *acceptance*—not for *servanthood* (i.e., the service and sacrifice of Christ through us) to our spouse.

Perhaps this sounds a bit oversimplistic, but most engaged couples sincerely believe they will find value, purpose, and fulfillment through each other. Lawrence Crabb describes this as "justified self-centeredness" that usually remains hidden at the subconscious level.[13]

Because of our distorted cultural conditioning today, men entering marriage, for example, tend to place too high of a priority on sexual satisfactions, and women tend to place too high of a priority on material affluence. This "justified self-centeredness" is also often rooted in deep-seated personal skepticism. Most bridegrooms—despite the outward "macho image" they sport—are usually somewhat lacking in self-confidence. They really wonder if they are able to fully meet their marital responsibilities. Most brides enter marriage having been "culturally conditioned" to be somewhat *suspicious and untrusting of men*—despite their genuine love for their husbands. *Each partner enters marriage lacking full affirmation as an individual, and they immediately begin to seek that affirmation from their spouse.*

We have already learned that our needs for acceptance and fulfillment can only be accomplished by Christ indwelling us; our spouses cannot do it. It is only inevitable that we each fail to provide all that our spouses need from us. Add specific dysfunctionally-rooted reactions of early traumatic events, and the underlying embedded emotional empowerments of our self-seeking and self-protecting, and the *downward spiral starts.*

The more we are disappointed in what are perceived to be life-threatening ways, the more we tend to *distance ourselves* from our life-partners to protect ourselves from further "life-threatening" hurts. Apart from genuine inner heart healing and love-motivated servanthood, this cycle of "if you hurt me, I'll hurt you" goes on in an unbroken circle. Many married couples "wake up" seven years and three children later into the marriage, only to find that their hurts are so deeply ingrained and their weariness is so overwhelming that the ability to salvage things appears hopeless. Despair sets in. This happens to

Christians and non-Christians alike. We may accept part of the blame, but we can't see where we failed. Meanwhile, God seems to be 25 light-years away.

The social isolation that has become part of today's mobile culture has made our spouses an even more vital source for our individual sense of fulfillment, confidence, and well-being. This applies especially to women. Dr. James Dobson has often mentioned in his radio program that husbands in past generations have *never* fully met their wives' expectations in the areas of homemaking and child-raising. But this has now become a major issue among wives today because our culture has eliminated the support groups that wives and mothers had with other women in the past! With the support and affirmation from these groups taken away, wives today look more than ever to their husbands for that support.

Men derive self-esteem by being respected, and women feel worthy when they are appreciated and loved. That poses a serious problem, since most women cannot genuinely respect men today because men have for many years now failed to meet their wives' perceived needs. Most wives want their men to be both *men of strength of conviction* (versus being a "wimp"), and *men of compassion* (versus being emotionally "cold"). The fact is that it is very difficult for most men to provide their wives with that *proper balance* (especially with the handicap of their own dysfunctionally-rooted drives). That proper balance differs from woman to woman, and without patient communication with his wife, a husband may never know what his wife's specific preferences are. This deep level of patient communication almost never exists at the start of a marriage; it must be carefully developed over time. The adjustment process needed to develop this communication and to learn each other's preferences and tendencies is both vital and difficult.

Again, it is humanly impossible for husbands and wives to meet one another's needs without help from the indwelling Holy Spirit of Christ Jesus. No husband can continue indefinitely to genuinely appreciate and love a wife who does not (or cannot) respect him for who he is and what he tries to do. Likewise, it is humanly impossible (without help from the indwelling Holy Spirit of Christ Jesus) for any wife to continue indefinitely to respect a husband who does not (or cannot) genuinely appreciate and love her for who she is.

This downward spiral is never one-sided, or even primarily one partner's fault. Robert Hicks contends that many wives today have unrealistic expectations of their husbands, just as much as husbands have of their wives. Though women want their husbands to be sensitive to their feelings, they are rarely able to be sensitive to their husband's feelings in turn:

Many women want men to be more feminine, but if they will admit it, they still want men to be strong in accordance with the older image. That's quite a bind for men! Women want men to be strong when they need strength, but they also want sensitive, caring males when they need those qualities. And of course, men have to guess which women want or need at any given moment. ...

Here's the rub. If men are now expected to do this because they love their wives and want to promote the psychological health of the marriage, women must [likewise] be able to handle the things men share. If a man's fears make his wife more fearful than the situation deserves, he probably won't continue to share his fears.

...men have had to learn to control their anger to be socially acceptable. But when the hidden rage of men is expressed to women, it is usually condemned.

Women can't have it both ways. If they want feelings, they are going to get male feelings, given and articulated in distinctively male ways. Women must learn to accept male feelings for what they are, no more and no less. Men have had to learn to accept female feelings for what they are. A woman's rejection of a man's feelings is just as counterproductive as a man's rejection of a woman's feelings. Feelings are not necessarily moral issues that need to be judged; they need to be listened to, understood, and considered significant.[14]

6. Healing the Downward Spiral

The only help for wounded and unsatisfying marriage relationships is inner heart healing from our dysfunctionally-rooted hindrances. But it takes more than one of the spouses walking through the deep repentance unto inner heart healing to save the marriage *per se*. That happens only when *both* spouses walk through it.

But when even one spouse receives healing, something very significant happens—those hurts are no longer "life-threatening," and the individual is freed to be Christ's vessel of love (as well as light and life) to the other. *That usually stops the downward movement of the spiral*, though it does not reverse it nor restore the marriage to full, beautiful soulical and spiritual harmony. But since the other spouse is no longer receiving "life-threatening" hurts from the first, there is reason for hope that the remaining spouse will indeed follow in time.

Christians do a fairly good job of coping with inner wounds on the surface. We try to apprehend Christ and His promises by faith; we ask Him to reveal areas of sin remaining in our lives; we attend seminars, conferences, and Bible studies about the marriage relationship, and we try to apply those lessons to ourselves. As a result, we have acquired some degree of communication and rapport, which relieves some of the pain. We also seek acceptance, appreciation, intimacy, and harmony in substitute activities to alleviate our frustrations. These include workaholism, substance addiction, Christian ministry, legalistic perfection, sports, physical fitness activities, etc. All the while, the hurts still linger deep down in our beings—and the pain continues to grow.

Most psychological counseling is powerless to get to those root causes and really help heal them. They address surface symptoms with treatment techniques that might give us another temporary respite from our pain. Even group therapeutic approaches can make us feel better for a while by helping us understand ourselves while providing a measure of acceptance by fellow Christians (though that is difficult for men). Unfortunately, as long as the root issues still run rampant, no matter how often our surface symptoms are addressed, it is inevitable that we will meet yet another crisis downstream.

Why wander and wait, when healing is available? Let us submit to Christian pastoral counseling for inner heart healing, where the indwelling Holy Spirit of Christ Jesus truly guides the counselor. Our first major adjustment predictably comes in the area of motives and personal expectations for the time of counseling. Most troubled couples come for counseling expecting the counselor to help *the other spouse* change his or her harmful ways. That's understandable! The only trouble is that that is not the Lord's way! He insists that we depend on Him to *change ourself*, regardless of what is done to change the other spouse (although He's after that too)!

But He is out to do far more than a healing of a marriage: He is out to root the sin out of our lives! Our Lord uses tribulations and challenges to actually *strengthen* our faith by forcing us to make hard commitment choices! He takes away all alternatives for our marriage relationships but two: (a) We can choose to *go all the way in Christ*, or (b) continue to *allow the marriage relationship to be destroyed*, with all lives involved suffering beyond our expectations. There is no third alternative.

7. What Is Going to Be Your Choice?

The choice to go "all the way" in Christ actually has four prongs to it. We must each unreservedly: (a) determine from here on to always respond to our spouses as Christ would have us, and not out of self-seeking and/or self-protecting; (b) act in expectation of His empowering us to so respond in all cases; (c) utterly abandon ourselves unto Him, depending upon Him to ensure that any results of our new ways are in our best interests; and (d) totally release our spouses to Him, that He alone, with no "help" from us, may deal with that spouse if and when He chooses!

We must each make that four-pronged choice separately from our spouse—whether or not our spouse ever does. This is a hard choice for most of us, but it is a choice we must make. If we don't, then by default we have made the choice of self, which leads to destruction! No fellow Christian, pastor, counselor, or spouse can crawl into our heads and make it for us! The crisis is too pressing for us to wait any longer—we must choose now!

If we choose the path of inner heart healing, we will have to commit ourselves to four things:

1. *Wives* must release the indwelling Holy Spirit of Christ Jesus to uproot and expose the buried emotional empowerments that drive them to *irrationally overreact* to life's frequent frustrations. These empowerments must be acknowledged, repented of, and surrendered to Christ on Calvary.

    Husbands must likewise release the indwelling Holy Spirit of Christ Jesus to uproot and expose the buried emotional empowerments that drive them to withdraw.

2. *Wives* must be encouraged to draw so close to Christ as their "Tree of Life" and true source of acceptance, belonging, purpose, and fulfillment, that they no longer look to their husbands to provide those most foundational human spiritual needs.

    Husbands must be encouraged to draw so close to Christ as their "Tree of Life" and true source of acceptance, belonging, purpose, and fulfillment, that they no longer look to their wives to provide those most foundational human spiritual needs.

3. *Wives* must learn to truly respect their husbands in response to their love, as Christ's children respect Him in response to His love (see Eph. 5:22-25).

    Husbands must learn to truly love their wives, as Christ loves His Church (see Eph. 5:22-25).

Note: The third step is impossible until considerable progress is first made in the previous two steps. That is where the inner heart healing process in both partners is essential to healing the hurt, and to reversing the downward spiral.

8. Especially for Men

Behold, I am going to send you Elijah the prophet before the coming of the great and terrible day of the Lord. And he will restore the hearts of the fathers to their children, and the hearts of the children to their fathers, lest I come and smite the land with a curse (Malachi 4:5-6).

Many excellent books have become available in recent years that address the emotional and spiritual hurts of women, especially Christian wives! They show women how they can obtain encouragement and strength through Christ. But *how about men*? Until very recently, there was very little done to effectively address the corresponding masculine issues, even though men—especially husbands and fathers—have a major impact, for good or for evil, on their families. Now, however, four excellent books are available that address such deep masculine issues, especially the powerful influences that fathers have over their sons and daughters. Any negative influences impact those children all throughout their adult lives unless dealt with by inner heart healing.

God gave husbands and fathers the responsibility to provide peace, love-security, and compassion in the marriage relationship, and to properly affirm daughters as women and sons as men. Why? God created the man with an "aura" related to his masculinity, which exudes a subtle but strong power to influence most women, sons, daughters, and other younger men. This is the anointing to lead.

He has that anointing unless he abdicates his responsibility or abuses that power. Most men in our culture and in previous generations have abdicated their responsibilities or abused their power. The terrible curse in Malachi describes the result of this abdication and abuse. Those who do not allow the Lord to restore true and proper father-son relationships and heal our men's image of fatherhood are cursed.

I strongly recommend Gordon Dalbey's book, *Father and Son—The Wound, The Healing, The Call to Manhood,*[15] which addresses a father's impact on his sons. Dalbey focuses on the emotional, psychological, and spiritual damage men can inflict, specifically as a father to a son. The wounds are passed down from generation to generation, creating ever-present condemning voices that remind their victims they can never measure up as men. This epidemic affects the Church and society as a whole— it is a crisis of manhood. Many men are so wounded and afraid that they are in turn afraid to acknowledge both the masculine and feminine nature of God. Their fathers didn't teach them how to relate to women. Neither are they at peace with their jobs. They don't have a sense of calling about their work, and hence are unsure of themselves in their professions.

I also strongly recommend H. Norman Wright's *Always Daddy's Girl—Understanding Your Father's Impact On Who You Are.*[16] A daughter's relationship with her father—whether that relationship was wonderful, painful, or even non-existent—helps create the person she is today. Her career, relationships with men, and feelings about herself have all been shaped by a fallible father who may not have done a perfect job.

The book was primarily written to help adult women become healed of old hurts by enabling them to recognize their father's failures and weaknesses and why he responded the way he did. However, it should also be studied by fathers of still-young sons as well as daughters, to help them realize the powerful impact they have on children of both sexes.

Third, I strongly recommend a book published by the Minirth-Meier Clinic entitled, *The Father Book,*[17] an "instructional manual" for "coming to grips with being a dad." This practical book addresses in depth the role of fathers in the fathering process, and discusses how fathering differs from mothering. It covers the wide gamut of challenges a devoted Christian husband and father most probably will face at one time or another. It also delves into how to father in the difficult situations of divorce, separation, and remarriage.

Finally, I also strongly recommend Robert Hicks' book, *Uneasy Manhood—The Quest for Self-Understanding.*[18] This book explores in much detail the inner feelings, struggles, and fears of men as they try to relate to their many roles and responsibilities in our modern American culture.

The route to *inner heart healing*, though painful, is very worthwhile—but there is only one Source, only one Healing Fountain for our marriages and our relationships. We will find Him when we search for Him with our whole hearts (see Jer. 29:13).

End Notes: Chapter Nine

1. Goetting, Ann. "Divorce Outcome Research Issues and Perspectives." *Journal of Family Issues* 2 (1981): 350, 78.

2. Hetherington, Mavis. *Children and Divorce in Parent-Child Interaction: Theory, Research, and Prospects* R.W. Henderson, ed. (New York: Academic Press, 1981).

3. Longfellow, Cynthia. *Divorce in Context: Its Impact on Children in Divorce and Separation,* George Levinyer and O.C. Moles, eds. (New York: Basic Books, 1979).

4. Conway, Jim. *Adult Children of Legal Or Emotional Divorce: Healing Your Long-Term Hurt* (Downers Grove, IL: InterVarsity Press, 1990), p. 29. Copyright © 1990 Jim Conway. Used by permission of InterVarsity Press, P.O. Box 1400, Downers Grove, IL 60515.

5. Hammond, Frank and Ida. *Pigs in the Parlor* (Kirkwood, MD: Impact Books Inc., 1973), p. 123.

6. Hammond. *Pigs in the Parlor,* Ch. 21.

7. Payne, Leanne. *Crisis in Masculinity* (Wheaton, IL: Crossway Books, 1991).

8. Payne, Leanne. *The Broken Image* (Westchester, IL: Crossway Books, 1981; 14th printing 1990).

9. Dalbey, Gordon. *Father and Son—The Wound, The Healing, The Call to Manhood* (Nashville, TN: Thomas Nelson Publishers, 1992).

10. Wright, H. Norman. *Always Daddy's Girl—Understanding Your Father's Impact on Who You Are* (Ventura, CA: Regal Books, GL Publications, 1989).

11. Reisman, Judith A., Ph.D. *Soft Porn Plays Hardball—Its Tragic Effects on Women, Children and the Family* (Lafayette, LA: Huntington House Publishers, 1991).

12. Soft pornography surely doesn't appear to be "soft" in my opinion. "Soft" here has a purely "technical" definition of not depicting actual acts of coitus, beyond that, obviously "anything goes"!

13. Crabb, Lawrence J., Jr. *Men & Women—Enjoying the Difference* (Grand Rapids, MI: Zondervan Publishing House, 1991).

14. Hicks, Robert. *Uneasy Manhood—The Quest for Self-Understanding* (Nashville, TN: Oliver Nelson Division, Thomas Nelson Publishers, 1991), pp. 31-33. Copyright © 1991. Used by permission of Thomas Nelson Publishers. All rights reserved.

15. Dalbey. *Father and Son.*

16. Wright, H. Norman. *Always Daddy's Girl.*

17. Minerth, Dr. Frank; Dr. Brian Newman; and Dr. Paul Warren. *The FATHER Book* (Nashville, TN: Thomas Nelson Publishers, 1992).

18. Hicks, Robert. *Uneasy Manhood—The Quest for Self-Understanding* (Nashville, TN: Oliver Nelson Division, Thomas Nelson Publishers, 1991).

Chapter Ten

Some Particular Dysfunctionally-Rooted Cases

We now address several common examples of dysfunctionally-rooted traumatic cases and their resulting self-protecting strategies.

1. Dysfunctionally-Rooted Effects Down to the Fourth Generation

Even if a couple stays together as a married couple for social or financial reasons, they can be *emotionally* divorced. Consider what the downward spiral of dysfunctionally-rooted behavior and its distancing does to the children of a marriage. It is utterly impossible for them to keep their children from suffering because of that reality.

One of the most thorough references on this topic is a book by Jim Conway entitled, *Adult Children Of Legal Or Emotional Divorce—Healing Your Long-Term Hurt.*[1] I strongly recommend this book for every parent to study carefully. Divorce horribly and dysfunctionally affects children, even if the divorce is "only" emotional and not legal.

In order to survive, the "children of divorce" themselves develop specific self-protecting strategies in reaction to the pain of parental, legal or emotional divorce. These strategies closely parallel those of children of alcoholic parents. Conway writes:

In addition to taking on extra jobs to keep the family together, children often assume other roles that help them survive in their troubled family. Claudia Black, author of a number of articles about the children of alcoholics, has observed that many children try very hard to look good or to be people-pleasers, while other children become delinquents. Most children adopt one or a combination of the following roles: the responsible one, the hero, the adjuster, the lost child, the placater, the scapegoat, or the mascot.[1,2]

Conway continued to expand the characteristics of these "roles" adopted by children trying to survive the trauma of divorce in the home:

The responsible one acts very mature and responsible beyond his or her years. ... These children, referred to by others as the hero type, are usually the firstborn in the family and compensate for family weaknesses. These kids appear to be well adjusted, high achiever, and overall very successful.

The second role many children play is that of the adjuster. This child adjusts by detaching. ... Sometimes the adjuster is referred to as the lost child. The lost child spends a lot of time in his or her room, playing alone, and feeling lonely. This child is the forgotten child. He or she tends to be shy, withdrawn and quiet. These children will follow anyone's suggestion. They seem afraid or incapable of making decisions. They think, "it doesn't matter." They have no sense of themselves and they believe that they cannot change their environment or their own lives.

Some children are also placaters who are very sensitive and automatically try to reduce tension in any situation. They work hard at taking care of everyone's feelings and needs—everyone's except their own.

... The scapegoat absorbs all of the family faults and may become the black sheep of the family by getting involved in drugs, alcohol, illicit sex, stealing and overall failure. Unconsciously, the dysfunctional family projects all of the family guilt and failure onto this person. The scapegoat is often the second child.

The purpose of the mascot is to reduce tension by doing or saying something funny. Typically, he or she is the family clown or goof-off. The responsibility is to distract people from the family's dysfunction. Unfortunately, mascots are marked by avoidance, hyperactivity, the inability to wrestle with hard problems. They usually are very uncomfortable if they are required to share their feelings or to be with people who are sharing their feelings.

Children take on these roles as a way to find a secure place in a chaotic environment. Acting out a part gives a feeling of reality and identity. But many of these children don't find out for many years that they have been only playing roles, not living life. Whenever a person plays a role, it indicates a problem with trusting people.[3]

Claudia Black delineates these in greater detail in her popular book, *It Will Never Happen To Me*[4]. Although the first three "roles" appear to be "good" on the surface, children who adopt any of these roles intrinsically learn to never talk, trust, or share their true inner emotions with others. *Emotional distancing—even with loved-ones*—is a primary characteristic of all adult children of alcoholics. The same is true of the "children of divorce." They never discover what they want themselves, so they never seek or find their own inner value, beauty, and purpose. They never trust others, and find it impossible to get close enough to anyone to receive care, concern for them, or to find intimacy. Loneliness, depression, and a sense of worthlessness are their constant companions. Sadly, they inadvertently tend to impose those very same dysfunctional syndromes on their own children.

2. Abuses and Disintegration of Dignity and Self-Image

We have mentioned that the pain of rejection, lack of identity, and non-affirmation leads to extremely destructive dysfunctionally-rooted behavior patterns ranging from downward disintegration of the marriage relationship (due to distancing from loved ones) to sexual perversions. But what about those cases where the root dysfunctional causes are *compounded by dignity-destroying abuse*? It is amazing that such people even survive to adulthood with such deep wounds and strong self-protecting strategies!

Perhaps the most common and widespread form of dysfunctionally-caused trauma in America today is *verbal abuse*. Like all other forms of abuse, it leaves emotional scars that impact its abused victims throughout their adult lives, unless it is dealt with through inner heart healing. Verbal abuse may not leave visible bruises, but *the ugly wounds and scars are there nonetheless.* If words pierced your heart as a child, if they have wounded your marriage or sent your career into a tailspin, *you may be a victim of verbal abuse.*

Dr. Grace Ketterman's book, *Verbal Abuse—Healing the Hidden Wound,*[5] offers invaluable insights to help readers learn how to deal with their pain so their wounds can be healed. Dr. Ketterman explains what verbal abuse sounds like, and helps readers determine if they've been wounded by it so they can start on the road to emotional and spiritual recovery. She also explores the types of family systems that perpetuate verbal abuse. She lists telltale symptoms to help readers determine if they themselves are abusers.

Most abusers are unaware that they are causing such emotional pain on their own victims, and therefore are unaware that they are abusers themselves. Most abusers were also victims of verbal abuse back one or more generations. Ketterman's book is of great value not only to adult victims of verbal abuse, to guide them in their own healing as we just said; it is also an important book for parents of young children, to help them recognize and break dysfunctional patterns of verbal abuse before they are passed down to yet another generation.

Childhood sexual abuse is alarmingly widespread. I strongly recommend Dan Allender's book on this subject, *The Wounded Heart—Hope For Adult Victims Of Childhood Sexual Abuse.*[6] Sexual abuse can take the form of either verbal and/or physical acts. Since our personhood is intrinsically linked to our sexuality paradigms, sexual abuse may be defined as whatever abuse attacks our personhood, particularly our sense of identity as male or female persons. Sexual abuse destroys our sense of personal worth, value, and personal dignity. Allender points out that *purely verbal* sexual abuse can be almost as devastating as abuse with a physical element:

> Sexually abusive words produce the same damage as sexually abusive contact.

> ...all inappropriate *sexual* contact is damaging and soul-distorting. *Seventy-four percent* of the least-severely abused victims report severe damage later in life.

> Sexual abuse is damaging no matter how the victim's body is violated.[7]

> Seventy-four percent! Wow!

Traumatic sexual abuse causes many dysfunctionally-rooted problems, particularly *shame* and *distrust*. *Shame* is anger directed toward oneself; *distrust* is anger directed toward others, especially to those of the same gender of the abuser.

Guilt is a major component of the emotional power behind those dysfunctionally-rooted distortions. The vast majority of all sexual abuse victims are abused by beloved adults (i.e., by a father in incest). That causes the abused victims to blame themselves *for at least having some part in the act or words of the abuse*. Allender points out that *this most frequently occurs in a family environment where the parent or parents are already failing to provide the normal love-nurturing to the child in the first place.*[8] Children in such an environment are starved for the normal attention they *should have been receiving* from their parents. Therefore, when a trusted adult normally respected by the child makes overtures of attention, the child is "naturally" drawn into it. In addition, the child has *intrinsic respect* for the abusing adult and tends to "*defend*" him or her, and to personally *assume the blame*.

This deep sense of *shame and self-abnegation* is perhaps the most difficult part of the dysfunctionally-rooted distortions to be healed of during the inner heart healing process. But imagine the following scenario:

> Suppose that God decreed the room you are in is to remain in darkness for the next five minutes, and has clearly communicated that command in a way everyone fully understands.

> But in deliberate and open rebellion I (the abuser) throw the light switch on the wall. What happens? The electric bulb in the overhead light fixture bathes the room in the God-forbidden light.

> Does that mean the bulb has sinned? No, of course not. The bulb is only responding the way it was made to respond. It was engineered, designed, manufactured, and installed to light up when electricity is turned on. Therefore, I, the abuser who threw the switch, am fully responsible for the sin—not the electric bulb.

The same is true of a female child sexually abused by an older man. God carefully engineered, designed, manufactured (created), and "installed" the girl for the purpose of *servanthood as a woman.* He purposely equipped her with drives, longings, and physical faculties for that servanthood. When an older man, in open sin, draws her, she is only responding in accordance with the way she has been "fearfully and wonderfully made" (Psalms 139:14). That is why *God always holds the man responsible for sins of adultery*, even when the woman fully cooperates!

3. Loss, Grief, and the Grieving Process

Some of the most traumatic events we experience, which often trigger dysfunctionally-rooted reactions, involve the *loss of someone or something very dear and close to us—* the death of a spouse or another loved one, divorce, or the loss of our health, our job, or financial security.

Psychologists have studied this aspect of suffering and have established a model with several distinct stages we tend to experience when we go through such a loss. That model is commonly known as "The Grieving Process."

Elisabeth Kubler-Ross first codified "The Grieving Process" as a result of extensive interviews with terminally ill hospital patients (primarily suffering with cancer) and their families.[9] She observed five psychological stages such patients experienced:

1.   Denial[10]

2.   Anger with both depression and hope

3.   Bargaining

4.   Preparatory depression

5.   Acceptance

In the more than 20 years since it was first published, these stages of "The Grieving Process" have been applied, with much modification and redefinition, to a broad spectrum of psychological traumas involving loss, whether it was of a person, a thing, or of some ability which is dear to us personally. Various psychologists and authors have used slightly different models and terms to label the stages. For example, J. William Worden lists "Four Tasks of Mourning" as follows:

Task I: To Accept the Reality of the Loss—the facts of the loss, the meaning of the loss, or the irreversibility of the loss (referring to T.L. Dorpat[11]).

Task II: To Experience the Pain of Grief—the literal physical pain, the emotional pain, and the behavioral pain.

Task III: To Adjust [not to the loss *per se,* but] *to an Environment in Which the Deceased Is Missing*—in such a way that it can rebound to the benefit of the survivor.

Task IV: To Withdraw Emotional Energy and Reinvest It in Another Relationship—or attachment; this often takes 2 to 4 years.[12]

In this same reference, Worden also lists many common manifestations of grief, categorized in (a) emotional feelings; (b) physical sensations; (c) cognitions; and (d) behaviors.[13]

In a book published by the Minirth-Meier Clinic Series, *Love Is A Choice, six* stages are discussed: (a) shock and denial; (b) anger; (c) depression; (d) bargaining and magic; (e) sadness; and (f) forgiveness, resolution, and acceptance.[14]

These four, five, or six-stage models illustrate, in perhaps an oversimplified way, how we dysfunctionally react to traumas and how we can obtain deliverance through the inner heart healing process. Our acquisition of self-protecting strategies and their emotional empowerment closely correspond to the second and third stages of the Kubler-Ross model, and the repentance steps of the inner heart healing process could correspond closely to the fourth and fifth stages.

Let us now briefly examine this model in light of inner heart healing from dysfunctionally-rooted distortions. But we must take caution to *avoid excessive reliance on the model.* In actual practice, the steps considerably overlap and often repeat over time; they do not necessarily follow the simple one-through-five sequence that is implied. Second, the full significance and intricacy of each step cannot be captured by the single word or label often used to define steps in the model. Third and most importantly, the model does not, in its published discussions, introduce *the necessity of repentance-surrender unto Christ Jesus* for final recovery. Finally, it is not true that we will "automatically" complete all five stages if we persist long enough (i.e., on our own efforts). Final victory through the last two steps is only possible through yielding to the indwelling Holy Spirit of Christ Jesus, as one's Tree of Life, during the inner heart healing process.

By incorporating our biblical and spiritual understanding, we have developed a more complete model of the five stages of "The Grieving Process": (a) shock; (b) acquisition of self-protecting goals and strategies; (c) acquisition of emotional empowerment; (d) repentance of self-protecting goals and strategies; and (e) repentance of their emotional empowerment. (The corresponding labels in secular psychology are (a) denial[15]; (b) anger with both depression and hope; (c) bargaining; (d) grief/emptying; and (e) acceptance.)

Shock (Denial[16])

Shock is our first reaction to any traumatic event. It is a means of self-protection that keeps us from overreacting to the immediate crisis. Shock has considerable physiological aspects which we do not discuss here. But its psychological aspects include *incredulity* ("I can't believe this has happened!" or simply, "Oh no!"). *Numbness* then sets in, and we act as if the event had not actually occurred (to whatever extent circumstances permit). Obviously, the labels "denial" or "disbelief" do indeed fit.

Acquisition of Self-Protecting Goals and Strategies (Anger Accompanied With Both Depression and Hope)

When we finally become mentally aware of reality, our reaction varies according to our particular personality quirks. The more aggressive among us *fight back* in anger, while the rest of us simply *withdraw and plan more determined reactions.* In either case, we bring our *natural strength* to bear to try to *reverse* the effects of the loss. When a spouse dies, many of us want to run, to find a substitute replacement, or to become engrossed in activities that distract us from the reality that a significant part of ourselves is gone.

It is at this stage that self-protecting goals and self-protecting strategies become established, usually without our conscious awareness. Fearing that the hurts will be repeated in the future, we establish behavioral strategies to prevent similar events from reoccurring, or to remain emotionally detached from them. Fears of failure and exposure of one's inadequacies also may drive one to develop extensive self-protecting strategies.

Acquisition of Emotional Empowerment Thereto (Emotional Resistance, Possibly With "Bargaining")

Next, or perhaps at the same time, we also become emotionally aware of the deeply frustrating results of the traumatic event. Again, our reaction depends upon our particular personality quirks. The more aggressive among us *vent our frustrations* on anything or anyone available: our spouse, the dog, our boss, coworkers, etc. The rest of us go into *depression and despair.*

Since our reactions to the loss are now primarily driven by our *emotions*, our behavior takes on *irrational aspects.* We may try to "bargain" with God: "I'll do such-and-such if You'll [temporarily] restore my loss." Some of us may follow the route of obsessive behaviors such as chemical abuse or sexual deviancy. Others may totally withdraw, and perhaps go into deep despair or depression.

At this stage, our self-protecting goals and self-protecting strategies become emotionally embedded and empowered—almost always without our conscious awareness.

Repentance of Self-Protecting Goals and Strategies (Grief and Emptying)

Sooner or later reality impacts us a second time. We begin to realize, at least mentally, how negatively all of this is affecting our lives and well-being, and we generally seek help. We may not know where or to whom to turn, but we begin to realize that we are in a helpless situation, one from which we are unable to recover. So, as consciously as we can, *we stop struggling by our own efforts*. We empty ourselves of our futile self-efforts as much as we can, and try to at least get some rest. But our self-protecting goals and strategies and their underlying emotional empowerment are hidden from our awareness due to denial.

At this point, Christians should yield to the first five essential commitments of the inner heart healing process described in Chapter Eight. Inner heart healing requires total surrender to our Lord Christ Jesus.

Surrender of Their Emotional Empowerment (Acceptance)

Part of the process of *abandoning our own efforts* so we can find rest and perhaps some outside help, is *our acceptance of the full reality of our loss* so we can reestablish our lives. This may happen as we develop new involvements or find a genuine replacement for the thing or loved one we lost. At the very least, we resolve to choose, in mental discipline, to remove ourselves from the loss as much as possible.

At this stage, Christians who have suffered such a traumatic loss must move on to the last three yielding steps in the inner heart healing process described in Chapter Eight. Only then can our Lord Christ Jesus within us bring us ultimate victory.

4. Dysfunctionally-Rooted Distortions of Compulsive Masturbation

Earlier in Chapter Three, I strongly emphasized the point that masturbation is not a viable way to handle the physical sex drive for "Spirit-filled" Christians—whether they are single or married.

Compulsive masturbation deserves additional examination for several reasons. First, it is perhaps the *most common and widespread example of sexual disfunctionality* today. It may even be one of the most widespread "secret sins" of Bible-believing Christians.[17] Second, it is perhaps the *most difficult form of bondage* from which to win freedom—even for Christians. Third, compulsive masturbation is typical of a class of inner bondage forms where *physical pleasure is used to temporarily relieve the pain of inner emptiness*—without the guilt of immediate moral irresponsibility. (Gluttony and some forms of substance abuse are also included in this class of inner bondages).

Habitual masturbation is a sexual dysfunction, and it is very destructive to the marriage relationship for a number of reasons:

1. Habitual masturbation seeks pleasure apart from moral responsibility. It is rooted in the *self-seeking protective goals* of:

    a. temporarily relieving the inner pain of insecurity and rejection; and

b. distancing oneself to avoid the inner pain of rejection by a real or hypothesized spouse. Habitual masturbation is particularly destructive to the marriage relationship because it powerfully reinforces this *distancing* tendency.

2. It is a habit that causes a paradigm to become rooted in us that distorts our views of the opposite sex. That in turn makes it even more difficult to ever attain to the God-ordained marriage relationship described throughout this book.

3. Even in an otherwise "Christian" marriage, masturbation gives rise to a serious unbalance in our view of human sexuality: It gives the sex drive far too much emphasis, at the expense of the ministry of love, tenderness, and encouragement of Christ to our spouse.

4. It is without Christ, and hence an area of spiritual darkness. Thus it is an open invitation for satan and his horde of demons to harass us. Once that starts to happen, it is even a far more difficult uphill battle for us than the mental discipline of avoiding sexual arousal in the first place.

5. If not stopped, that satanic harassment inevitably leads to deeper and deeper sexual deviancy, adultery, homosexuality/lesbianism, or even more horrible perversion. Indeed, we prophesy that any "Spirit-filled" Christian walking in any of these areas of darkness will, with virtual certainty, end up in captivity by either the spirits of homosexual depravity or the spirits of Jezebel in these days of spiritual warfare now facing us!

6. Even if we keep satan off, it is still a pampering of the flesh. The flesh can never be satisfied; the more we pamper our flesh, the more it demands. Hence masturbation quickly becomes an increasingly demanding habit! And it is perhaps the most difficult habit to break, even more difficult than habits of substance abuse.

Chronic masturbators make the superficial choice to obtain pleasure and temporary relief from unreleased sexual arousal while protecting themselves from the possible pain of being rebuffed during intimacy with a real "significant other." They believe they can obtain this pleasure and relief (and protection) without the *guilt* of moral irresponsibility to the "significant other."

Married partners who engage in chronic masturbation often develop the powerful self-protective goal and strategy of distancing themselves from their spouses for *self-protection against that pain* (i.e., of sexual rejection). This *amplification of distancing* for self-protection helps make chronic masturbation especially harmful in the marriage relationship, especially when coupled with a lack of mutual communication about sex.

There is a very close link between *eros* love or sexual passion on one hand, and *spiritual* influences on the other. That is why the sexually deviant practices of heterosexual adultery, homosexuality, monosexualism (masturbation), and psychopathic sadism are so *prevalent among satan worshipers and New Age followers*, and are also so frequent among "spiritual" Christians (to the shock of many). The more a person's soul (including the mind and emotions) is sensitive to and yielding to *spiritual influences*[18], the more *vulnerable* that person is to *eros* love or sexual passion! This is somewhat ironic. Unless those spiritual influences are constrained by the indwelling Holy Spirit of Christ Jesus, sexual sins, distortions, and deviances are likely to result.

This tight link between sexual passion and spiritual influences nearly always ensures the presence of demonic reinforcement of sexually deviant practices, *including chronic masturbation.* Since these practices involve the strongest of fleshly drives, they are, as habits, easily reinforced demonically. Satan is always quick to send his demonic spirits to reinforce our dark thinking patterns (i.e., all thoughts not fully consistent with the will of the indwelling Christ). This is particularly true for sins of sexual deviance; chronic masturbation is definitely included in this category, though it perhaps appears to be "mild" compared to most other forms of sexual perversion. The strong demonic power involved here makes it particularly mandatory that a total and decisive submission be made of the behavior habits and its underlying self-protecting goals and strategies to Christ indwelling. Only the power of Christ indwelling is sufficient to break the bondage!

Sexual pleasure without accountability is *not* the *root* cause for chronic masturbation, however; so it doesn't by itself offer us a clue as to how to overcome it. One of the real root issues is the abnormal seeking for an identity as a person (whether as a male or a female). The dysfunctional root cause in the vast majority of cases is *low self-esteem resulting from a lack of proper affirmation as masculine or feminine!*

Another root cause of chronic masturbation, often related to this, is dysfunctionally-rooted loneliness. This leads to chronic masturbation when the denial of the dysfunctional roots is accompanied by an undisciplined fantasy life in the mind. Male sexual incitement (i.e., intense sexual drive) goes far beyond mere seminal fluid pressure,

sexual arousal or excitement, all of which are often triggered by the visual sexual stimuli so common in our culture today. Incitement comes from *using fantasy to avoid
the emotional pain and physical discomfort* when those
pressures or excitements are not properly released. The
female counterpart comes from *using fantasy to alleviate
what appears to be hopeless loneliness.* In either case, this
form of bondage becomes extremely destructive when
fantasy amplifies the otherwise normal sexual drives.

Yet another "reason" is *depression.* Masturbation may
appear to provide the only "pleasure" possible when life
appears to be hopelessly joyless. Patterns of chronic masturbation often begin when an individual feels trapped
for life in an offensive life style, or where life offers little
hope for true happiness. Such deep depression or despair
itself almost always has dysfunctional roots. It may even
be tied in with a "mid-life crisis," or some other problem.
This problem is characteristic in a high portion (we
estimate as high as 60 percent or more) of married Christian men in America today. It is also particularly prevalent in today's rootless and commuter culture.

In either case, final inner heart healing of this chronic
problem requires (a) completion of the inner heart healing process through totally involved repentance of every
aspect of our sin-nature that bears on it; and (b) finding
full affirmation as persons through our personal relationship with Christ Jesus.

Only when Christ becomes the source of our root
needs, and our scapegoat for its emotional empowerment,
do we become free from the "need" for such masochistic
pleasure. A deliberate choice on our part is vital here. Victory requires us to consciously, deliberately, and persistently choose the correct basic goal of handling our inner
sense of emptiness, lovelessness, and insecurity through
dynamic faith in the indwelling Christ.

Christ as our Tree of Life

5. Terrible Curses on Vietnam Veterans

Even though we may suffer from severely painful and dysfunctionally distorted reactions to rejection, lack of sexual identity as persons, abuse, loss of personal dignity, or loss of a loved one or possession, probably the *most painful and dysfunctionally distorted reactions known today* are those resulting from *direct involvement in warfare, massacres, or other disasters.* This is a common experience of virtually every person who saw military service in the Vietnam War.

Many things unique to the Vietnam War *combined* to form an especially traumatic experience for American soldiers involved in the conflict:

1. The Vietnam War was apparently totally meaningless and without purpose. *No satisfactory reason was ever given for it,* and most of our soldiers perceived that *the local populace resented our fighting "for them."* (One author, Arvo Manhattan, even argues with much documentation that our real reason was religious: to keep the power a Roman Catholic government system over a Buddhist majority populace.[19])

2. There was a gross waste of human life involved in the Vietnam War.

3. The individual soldier's attitude of being there was not to achieve some military victory, but *simply to survive for 365 days.*

4. *Americans back home almost totally rejected the soldiers* as they returned home.

5. There was a *total lack of debriefing* upon the soldiers' return to the United States. This left them totally unprepared to resume civilian life, or

to deal with the deep hurts they suffered "on the killing fields."

The three key root hurts of most Vietnam War veterans were therefore: (a) *guilt,* for "surviving" when their close buddies did not, and for the lives they took in the meaningless killing: (b) *loss of identity and purpose* in life—the vast majority of them were plunged into the meaningless mess of Vietnam at the critical time of their lives (age 18), the time when they normally would be affirmed as men with value and dignity, as persons with a purpose and goal in life. They were then plunged back into American life without debriefing, at a time when they desperately needed to be retaught proper social values; and (c) *rejection by the folks back home* for taking part in such an unpopular and sinful war (even though most had no choice in the matter, and those who did were deceived by national leaders). What a devastating combination of dysfunctional hurts!

Two references provide a great deal of understanding and insight into the horrible depths of Post-Traumatic Stress Disorder (PTSD), as the Veteran's Administration calls it, and its root causes and most common manifestations. They include Chuck Dean's book, *Nam Vet—Making Peace With Your Past,*[20] and *America Ambushed!—The Unseen War.*[21] Both publications are available through a ministry (Point Man International Ministries) that was establish specifically to help Vietnam War veterans.[22] The first book is evangelistic in its purpose, and primarily details the causes and nature of PTSD. The second book delineates the *spiritual curses* deliberately placed on all Americans in Vietnam by Buddist priests[23] and how in Christ, victory can be obtained.

End Notes: Chapter Ten

1. Conway, Jim. *Adult Children of Legal or Emotional Divorce: Healing Your Long-Term Hurt* (Downers Grove, IL: InterVarsity Press, 1990).

2. Black, Claudia. "Innocent Bystanders at Risk: The Children of Alcoholics," *Alcoholism* 1:3, pp. 22-26 in Conway, *Adult Children of Legal or Emotional Divorce.* See also Sharon Wegscheider-Cruse, *Another Chance: Hope and Health for the Alcoholic Family* (Palo Alto, CA: Science and Behavior Books, 1981).

3. Conway, Jim. *Adult Children of Legal or Emotional Divorce,* pp. 99-100. Copyright © by Jim Conway. Used by permission of InterVarsity Press, P.O. Box 1400, Downers Grove, IL 60515.

4. Black, Claudia. *It Will Never Happen to Me: Children of Alcoholics as Youngsters—Adolescents— Adults* (New York: Ballentine Books, 1981).

5. Ketterman, Grace H., M.D. *Verbal Abuse—Healing the Hidden Wound* (Ann Arbor, MI: Servant Publications, 1992).

6. Allender, Dan. *The Wounded Heart—Hope for Adult Victims of Childhood Sexual Abuse* (Colorado Springs, CO: NavPress, 1990).

7. Allender. *The Wounded Heart,* pp. 33,31,36. Copyright © 1990 by Dan B. Allender. Used by permission of

NavPress, Colorado Springs, CO. All rights reserved. For copies call 1-800-366-7788.

8. Allender. *The Wounded Heart,* pp. 33,31,36. Copyright © 1990 by Dan B. Allender. Used by permission of NavPress, Colorado Springs, CO. All rights reserved. For copies call 1-800-366-7788.

9. Kubler-Ross, Elizabeth, M.D., *On Death and Dying* (New York: Collier Books, Macmillan Publishing Company, 1969, 1st paperback ed. 1970).

10. This is not the same pschological concept of denial as discussed at the end of Chapter Eight.

11. Dorpat, T.L. "Suicide, loss and mourning," *Life-Threatening Behavior* 3 (1973), pp. 213-224.

12. Worden, J. William, Ph. D. *Grief Counseling and Grief Therapy —A Handbook for the Mental Health Practitioner* (Springer Publishing Company, Inc., New York 10012, 1982), pp. 17-18. Used by permission.

13. Worden, *Grief Counseling and Grief Therapy,* pp. 20-28. Used by permission.

14. Heinfelt, Dr. Robert, Dr. Frank Minirth, and Dr. Paul Merer. *Love Is a Choice* (Nashville, TN: Thomas Nelson Publication 1989), pp. 213-236.

15. This is not the same pschological concept of denial as discussed at the end of Chapter Eight.

16. This is not the same pschological concept of denial as discussed at the end of Chapter Eight.

17. Estimates are that in the continental United States in 1988, among Bible-believing Christians, about 60 percent of adult men and 30 percent of adult women were in bondage to chronic masturbation, even though

the majority were successful in keeping their bondage hidden from others. Actual numbers are probably within "plus-or-minus 10 percent" of these anedotal guestimates.

18. Either to demonic spirits or to the indwelling Holy Spirit of Christ Jesus.

19. Manhattan, Arvo. *Vietnam—Why Did We Go?* (Chino, CA: Chick Publications, 1984).

20. Dean, Chuck. *Nam Vet—Making Peace with Your Past* (Portland, WA: Multnomah Press, 1988).

21. *America Ambushed!—The Unseen War* (Compiled by the Veterans of Point Man International Ministries, Mountlake Terrace, WA, 1990).

22. Point Man International Ministries, P.O. Box 440, Mountlake Terrace, WA 98043 (Telephone: 206-486-5383).

23. Those three curses, which remarkably accurately describe the current state of most Vietnam War Veterans, were: (1) that the American soldiers would become wandering men for the rest of their lives; (2) that they would never find peace; and (3) that they would be angry men and women for the rest of their lives.

Part IV

Implications in Ministry

Up to now we have addressed human sexuality and self-seeking/protecting as they affect our individual relationships with Christ and our interpersonal relationships within marriage and with other people. We have stressed the need for every believer in Christ Jesus to walk through personal inner heart healing to remove the bondage of every self-seeking and self-protecting area of sin that so easily besets us. This need is especially grave for all who minister to other members of the Body of Christ.

We now address how that impacts on ministry.

Chapter Eleven

Self-Seeking and Self-Protecting Drives in Ministry

All true ministry in the Body of Christ is a form of *love-motivated servanthood*. It is only possible when it is empowered by the Spirit of Christ living within us, who distributes *His* light, life, love, and acceptance through us to others according to His will. True ministry can be defined as receiving from our Lord Christ Jesus and passing that on to others.

On the other hand, self-motivated ministry efforts in Christian denominationalism[1] represent a different paradigm or way of thinking. Even if these efforts are based on scriptural precepts, doctrines, or commandments, they are still *human efforts* to bring people into the protection and control of a "religious system" instead of a *vital relationship* with Jesus Christ. The Scriptures must always be our basis for all truth; but although many denominational churches and ministries teach God's word, our Christian denominations have not yet been fully purged of "living by the Tree (source) of Knowledge" (i.e., the law)!

1. Serving in Law by Self

Most Christians today—even "Spirit-filled" believers—still live in the second category. The "law" of the Scriptures (including the New Testament) is indeed of God; and it keeps us from being destroyed by our sins, according to Galatians 3:22-24! However, God's ultimate purpose is for us to yield to the living Christ and allow Him as Lord to do the living in and through us!

The primary qualification for true love-motivated servanthood (or ministry) is brokenness, which brings us to humility, meekness, patience, and utter abandonment unto our Lord Christ Jesus. The primary qualification for denominational ministry, on the other hand, is formal Bible schooling in knowledge of the Bible and of witnessing and preaching techniques. That knowledge is of course valuable; but it is *only a starting point* to lead us to Christ. Without brokenness, our ministries, as avenues of servanthood, manifest much of the *sin of self*. According to Romans 6:2-14, "self" is to be reckoned as dead—not manifested toward others in need! But without a vivid awareness of and utter abandonment unto *Christ in us*, we don't "dare" set "self" aside—it is the "driving force" behind our "ministry."

When we minister out of self, *nothing puffs up one's pride more than knowledge*—particularly knowledge that is both true and important (such as biblical truths). Such spiritual pride offers satan an opportunity to divert us and our ministries onto lesser issues and perhaps even to outright error! Either way, the Holy Spirit of Christ in us is considerably constrained when "self" rules the heart. Our intrinsic sexuality paradigms also play a major role in this.

Even without undue satanic distortions, men without Christ tend to *minister out of "delegated authority."* When satanic deception is strong—and it is a far too common situation—even well-meaning ministries *can do more harm than good* in the lives of God's people.

Ministry by the power of self, even when offered according to true scriptural knowledge rather than by Christ indwelling, significantly departs from love-motivated and Spirit-empowered servanthood in at least seven ways:

1. We assign incorrect priorities to the demands on our time.

2. We maintain our inner self-protecting barriers that distance ourselves from others (i.e., from those to whom we are to minister Christ's light, life and love).

3. We hold distorted views of human sexuality, and we retain unbiblical views of the roles of the opposite sex in the Body of Christ.

4. We act in presumption, erroneously thinking it to be faith because of the erroneous misunderstanding that Christ's authority is "delegated to us."

5. We evaluate fellow Christians in terms of their natural characteristics and abilities rather than in terms of *Christ in them.*

6. We cannot receive ministry from other members of the Body of Christ (except for a select few); therefore, we remain incomplete and unbalanced, lacking the fullness of Christ, and do not benefit from the checks and balances Christ has built into His Body.

7. We mistake soulishness for true spirituality, and fail in true spiritual discernment and wisdom.

⊀ 2. The Monster of Self in Ministry ⊁

The consuming "monster of self" is manifested in Bible-believing and Spirit-filled Christians in two ways: (a) *self-motivations* behind our ministries, and (b) *emphases made on law and denominationalism*. Regardless of the form, we must learn through experience (leading to brokenness) that *the life of self is totally impotent and insufficient*.

Self-motivation behind our ministries is very subtle, but its essence is our *intense need for finding fulfillment* through "serving God." Rick Joyner, commenting on Philippians 2:5-8, makes some powerful observations about this temptation:

> If we are to be true ministers we *must* heed the apostle's word...
>
> ...When we enter ministry with the intention of being filled and making a reputation, we have made a fundamental departure from true ministry. To repeat a most important exhortation for us all: "He who speaks from himself seeks his own glory (or recognition); but he who is seeking the glory of the One who sent him, he is true" [John 7:18].[2]

Our *self-centered approach* to "serving God" is not freedom, but bondage. Quoting Rick Joyner again, we read:

> The self-centered are not capable of attaining the higher principles of love, duty, justice, mercy, or even freedom—though they may vigorously preach these things. The self-centered may attach themselves to causes but the basic motivation of such

attachment will be self-centered.... The laying aside of personal ambition to become a true servant has become almost incomprehensible, yet this is precisely the course of the only true freedom we will ever know—becoming a servant of the Lord Jesus. Until He is the center of our life, we cannot know true sanity or true freedom.

...Those who truly know their God are the most confident, humble and peaceful people on earth....[3]

This applies to all other members of the Body of Christ as well as to our spouses. It is vital that we recognize the extent of the damage and havoc caused when we fail to truly allow *Christ in us* to live His life when and as He wills. *Our sin produces only emptiness and failure in all of our interpersonal relationships.*

Our personal insecurities cause us to keep ourselves distant from one another to avoid being hurt by criticisms, exhortations, admonitions, or anything else we don't want to hear! These inner distancing barriers severely impair our ability to genuinely love others in Christ and minister His love, acceptance, and significance to them. We do not get close enough to one another to really know each other's real needs and hurts well enough and deeply enough to pray, intercede, and minister effectively.

The only way to stop the otherwise inevitable deterioration of our interpersonal relationships is to *choose to embrace the pain* of inner heart healing. We must "tear down our walls and barriers" to allow Christ dwelling in us to minister His love, acceptance, and value to whomever to whom we are ministering—regardless of the personal cost to us. We must ultimately trust the faithfulness of the indwelling Christ to meet our needs for security and significance in the process, while cooperating with Him to demonstrate His faithfulness to those whom we love through practical acts of compassion and respect.

Why is this so hard for us to do? Many of us find it hard to really believe that Christ indwelling is indeed faithful Himself to meet our own personal needs for security and significance. This sin of unbelief drives us to seek these things by our own efforts, and to distance ourselves from others to avoid being hurt. The result of this unbelief is always more disappointment, more pain, more protective barriers, and more guilt.

But we must each choose to: (a) put aside our seeking for significance, fulfillment, and self-worth, and abandon ourselves utterly unto Him; and (b) tear down the inner barriers we have erected to keep from being hurt by others. This is the *"dying to the sin of self"* required of us in Romans 6:2-14. This is the only path to freedom that also demonstrates and witnesses the power of the "Christ in us" to others.

This way of life *demands a real death to self*, particularly to the internal barriers we have all erected for protection from hurt. When other members of the Body of Christ repeatedly demonstrate their failings, and utterly disappoint us, it is *hard* to trust in Christ enough to come into unity with them anyway!

⋇ 3. The Spirit of Baal ⋇

Two specific sexuality-related distortions of ministry directly result from *insecurity-driven* self-seeking. These two particularly destructive forms of evil spiritual influence in the Body of Christ are: (a) an abuse of authority we refer to as the *"darkness of Baal,"* and (b) a form of rebellion against authority that we call the *"darkness of Jezebel."* The male paradigm of human sexuality is particularly vulnerable to the first spiritual influence, and the female paradigm is particularly vulnerable to the second.

The "spirit of Baal" is a powerful and well-organized attempt by satan to *distort Christianity into a religion* "in the name of Christianity," but which actually puts people into bondage to him (satan). It is the driving force behind what the Bible calls "Babylon." This spiritual influence describes many aspects of modern "denominational Christianity" from which our Lord Christ Jesus is now working to deliver His Body. This very powerful evil spiritual force constantly attempts to distort Christianity *into a religion* that subtly serves satan, not Christ. Its primary methodology is to deceive leaders in the Body of Christ to *serve by the power of self* rather than by the in-dwelling Christ.

Satan has actively worked to distort Christianity into Baal since the first century under "Christian" titles. His strategy has been to do the following:

1. Replace the Body of Christ with denominationalism.

2. Distort the doctrines of biblical Christianity into unbiblical mystic elements.

3. Use those mystic elements to beguile "believers" and "leaders" to depend upon satan and his demonic spirits for strength and wisdom, while he and his demonic spirits in the meantime keep "hidden" behind those mystic elements.

4. Manipulate people to remain *loyal to the religious institution,* by giving people what they think they want (i.e., to be able to get away with sin and yet remain "saved") in exchange for their loyalty.

The particular paradigm of denominationalism is a key part of the spirit of Baal. Ministries in Christian denominationalism, even when based on scriptural precepts, doctrines, and commandments, are still *human* efforts to bring people into the protection and comfort of a religious system. Yes, it is ostensibly so they can be taught and led to salvation *via* Christ Jesus who died for us on Calvary. But it amounts to "living by the Tree (source) of Knowledge of Good and Evil" (dry, lifeless scriptural precepts—the "law"), rather than by the Tree of Eternal Life (the living, indwelling Christ Jesus).

⚹ 4. The Spirit of Jezebel ⚹

The "spirit of Jezebel" is a powerful and well-organized attempt by satan to *obtain direct dominating control of all leaders* within human organizations, including local Body of Christ gatherings and Christian churches. *It works through distortions and weaknesses of human sexuality.* This same spirit is the powerful force behind the obsessive sensuality, the open hatred for male authority, and the "women's liberation" and pro-abortion movements rampant in our society at large. It is closely associated with unbridled witchcraft (although that linkage has until now been kept well-hidden from the public). It also works very actively in Christian churches to destroy Christ's headship in the leadership ministries.

Jesus Christ personally warned Christians and churches against the spirit of Jezebel in Revelation 2:20-24. Christ spoke through John to the church in Thyatira (whose members were rich in deeds, love, faith, service, and perseverance):

> *But I have this against you, that you tolerate the woman Jezebel* [Greek: *Ietsabel*] *who calls herself a prophetess, and she teaches and leads*

My bond-servants astray, so that they commit acts
of immorality and eat things sacrificed to idols.
And I gave her time to repent; and she does not
want to repent of her immorality. Behold, I will cast
her upon a bed of sickness, and those who commit
adultery with her into great tribulation, unless they
repent of her deeds. And I will kill her children with
pestilence; and all the churches will know that I am
He who searches the minds and hearts; and I will
give to each one of you according to your deeds. But
I say to you, the rest who are in Thyatira, who do
not hold this teaching, who have not known the
deep things of Satan, as they call them—I place no
other burden on you (Revelation 2:20-24).

Jezebel is called "*a woman.*" This spirit or personality is identified in some way with the feminine sexuality paradigm. She acts as a "prophetess" and "teacher" to deceive fellow believers. She leads them into adultery and other immoral acts, but always in the context of religion ("things sacrificed to idols"). She is associated with the mystery of iniquity ("the deep things of Satan"), and we are to avoid being deceived by her.

The biblical type, of course, was the literal person named Jezebel (Hebrew: AYTs BL), the cruel Phoenician wife of Ahab, king of Israel. She also was the prophetess of the satanic religious system of Baal mentioned in First Kings 18–21 and Second Kings 9. But the passage in Revelation 2:20-24 refers to far more than the physical woman who died according to prophecy thousands of years ago—it refers to an evil spiritual force under satan! A study of the original Jezebel reveals many of the characteristics of the spiritual force operative today. We must never forget that we are dealing with a well-organized cadre of satanic demons who are out to distort the Body of Christ into a satan-serving religious organization.

This spirit of Jezebel is very active in Christian organizations as a "prophetess" and "teacher" to deceive fellow believers. Paul spoke sharply against her influences in the Body of Christ at Corinth. Many of the less disciplined local groups of the "Charismatic movement" of the 1960's and 1970's reflected many of her influences. The sexually-related sins that led to the downfall of certain well-known Christ-anointed television evangelists in the late 1980's also attest to her success!

This spirit is *intensely ambitious* in its attempts to *dominate and control people*. It controls individuals by manipulating people's emotions with a deadly combination of sexual lust, fear, guilt, and depression. It violently opposes all authority other than its own. It also works closely with the spirit of Baal, which is satan's counter religious system composed of people in spiritual bondage to him through distortion of the male sexuality paradigm.

Although the spirit of Jezebel and the spirit of Baal are actually genderless, their operations capitalize on gender-specific attributes and characteristics—especially weaknesses, needs, and hurts. The spirit of Jezebel particularly capitalizes on the feminine sexuality paradigm, and the spirit of Baal focuses on the male sexuality paradigm.

The spirit of Jezebel exerts a particularly strong temptation on Christian women who have discovered the incredible truth and power of their position in Christ, but who at the same time *reject the checks and balances in the Body of Christ*. These include the need for submission to the other believers in the Body as described in Ephesians 5:21. These checks and balances would automatically make such women aware of the insidious role of spiritual pride in their lives. Such women are especially vulnerable to spiritual pride due to the exceptional spiritual sensitivity they possess by virtue of their particular God-ordained sexuality paradigm.

Francis Frangipane discusses this propensity in some detail:

> ...the spirit of...Jezebel is more attracted to the uniqueness of the female psyche in its sophisticated ability to manipulate without physical force.

> ...[it] target[s] women who are embittered against men, either through neglect or misuse of authority. This spirit operates through women who, because of insecurity, jealousy or vanity, desire to control and dominate others. Jezebel is there behind the woman who publicly humiliates her husband [by her knowledge of her husband's particular weaknesses] with her tongue, and then thereafter controls him by his fear of public embarrassment.

> ...It is Jezebel who...[acerbates] dissatisfaction between spouses.

> ...There are respectable men who love God and who seek to serve Him, yet secretly in their hearts they are prisoners of Jezebel. Even now, they are deeply ashamed of their bondage to pornography; and they can barely control their desires for women.

> ...There are good women who come to church seeking God, but this spirit has them fantasizing about the men in the assembly; lamenting that their [own] husbands are not as "spiritual" as other husbands.

...Jezebel seeks the highly refined qualities of the professional musician[4], especially when such a man [or woman] has both the ambition and the opportunity to become a worship leader or director. ... Prayer leaders, church secretaries, worship and song leaders, pastors and their wives...are all especially targeted by this spirit.

...A woman can most certainly...be anointed by God to serve as a prophetess. But when she insists upon recognition, when she manipulates or entirely disregards the male leadership in the church, when she *"calls herself* a prophetess" [Rev. 2:20], beware.[5]

Because of the destructiveness and all-pervasiveness of this spirit satan is pouring out in an intense and highly focused assault on Christian believers, we must recognize it and take strong initiatives to wage spiritual warfare against it. Our main weapons are first of all the righteousness of Christ, followed by humility, faith, and prayer.

Again we quote various comments by Frangipane, this time about ways this spirit may be recognized and defeated:

Anyone [of us] who is hit by this spirit needs, first of all, to repent deeply of their sympathetic thoughts toward it, and then *war* against it! ... Pick up the sword of the Spirit [Ephesians 6:17—the Word of God] and war against the principality of Jezebel! ... War against Jezebel when you are tempted...that your aggressive counter attack is setting other people free!

...When you war against the principality of Jezebel, even though you stand against her lusts and

witchcrafts, you must guard against the power-demons of Fear and Discouragement, for these she will send against you to distract you from your warfare and your victory [as Jezebel did against Elijah in 1 Kings 19, and Herodias did against John the Baptist in Matthew 14]!

...The essence of pulling down strongholds [sin-nature thought pattern] [is] we destroy the defiling oppressive system of thinking which, through the years, has been built into our nature.

...When men assume God will not judge them, it is only a matter of time before the tempter comes to destroy them. ... The sin of presumption is the antithesis of the fear of the Lord. It is the harbinger of future defeat.

We cannot be successful in the heavenly war if we are not victorious in the battlefield of our minds. ... We cannot tolerate Jezebelian thinking in any area.[6]

End Notes: Chapter Eleven

1. Denominationalism is a paradigm or mentality of Christian religions wherein: (a) the Person of Christ indwelling is replaced by philosophy and theology based on doctrines about Him; (b) the social structure of the Body of Christ is replaced by a religious organization; and (c) the social dynamics of Body members ministering to one another is replaced by a priesthood-vs.-laity order in which one or a few elite "priests" or "ministers" do all the ministry, and the people provide the context and logistics for them. This error began to encrust Christianity before the end of the first century A.D., and by the mid-300's fully characterized the "visible" Christian Church. The Protestant reformation over the past 450 years has not yet completely weaned us from it.

2. Joyner, Rick. *The Harvest* (Pineville, NC: MorningStar Publications, 1989), p. 78.

3. Joyner, Rick. *There Were Two Trees In The Garden* (Pineville, NC: MorningStar Publications, 1986), p. 28.

4. This is a subtle but very important insight that Frangipane is sharing from personal experience and observation. It applies to all ministries that primarily deal with the *emotions* of people. The feminine sexuality paradigm is particularly active in such ministries; hence satanic deception in such cases would be much in line with this "spirit of Jezebel."

5. Frangipane, Francis. *The Three Battlegrounds— An In-depth View of the Three Areas of Spiritual Warfare: The Mind, The Church and the Heavenly Places* (Cedar Rapids, IA: Arrow Publications), pages 98-102. This book is available at Christian bookstores, or you may order directly from Arrow Publications, P.O. Box 10102, Cedar Rapids, IA 52410, or call 1-319-373-3011 using Master-Card or Visa.

6. Frangipane. *The Three Battlegrounds,* pp. 101-103, 106,112-113,117.

Chapter Twelve

Family vs. Ministry: Devastating Contentions

Our marriages and our lives as members of the Body of Christ will *inevitably remain in conflict* unless both are ordered according to the *Way of the cross*! Since most of us fall short in this area, we have to interpret the biblical teachings on both ministry and marriage in a purely legalistic sense, and we compromise each for the other in order to minimize the contention and sufferings of trying to do both.[1]

The *way of the cross* is a life style of love-motivated and Spirit-empowered servanthood that characterizes the New Testament Church. Our Lord Christ Jesus is bringing us to this life style, even though it is vastly different from the understandings of Christianity held by most Christians today. Few can understand it, and even fewer are truly ready for it. The most essential element of this *way of the cross* is to fully apprehend and yield to the indwelling Christ so He can live in and through us when and as He chooses. It is impossible to order our marriage relationships according to scriptural principles except through Christ in us. In the same way, it is also totally impossible to live as a functioning member of the Body of Christ except by faith through Christ in us.

1. Priorities

The subtle impacts of human sexuality and spiritual pride on ministries in the Body of Christ must also be studied so that we can understand how our Lord Christ Jesus is working to bring us unto true love-motivated and Spirit-empowered servanthood.

The very thought that God Himself has called us to a "ministry" has a powerful impact on the attitudes we have toward others. Pride subtly but quickly distorts our thinking, particularly with respect to our marriage partners: *After all, if I have this important task that the very God has called me to, then you must support me in it, or at least never hold me back! Doesn't the Bible say, "Wives, submit to your husbands"* We think we're doing God a favor![2]

Men tend to give highest priority to *constructive and meaningful accomplishments* (if not with their wives' mutual involvement, then without it). Women tend to give highest priority to *stability* and *security of life style* (particularly where children are involved—for which their husbands' mutual involvement is necessary). But when a man "knows" his calling or ministry in the Body of Christ, those relative priorities can be diametrically opposed!

Philippians 2:3 tells us clearly what our attitude should be toward others: "Do nothing from selfishness or empty conceit, but with humility of mind let each of you regard one another as more important than himself."

We need to have our personal priorities properly ordered according to biblical standards:

1. Our personal individual relationship with our Lord Christ Jesus.

2. Our spouse.

3. Our children.

4. Other family members.

5. Our job or "ministry."

Any other ordering considerably distorts our judgments on what His will is in the major decisions we make.

Most of us have no problem with the first priority, as a rule. Most believers in ministry, however, regard their families to be of a lower priority relative to the fulfillment of their "life goal" through their work or ministry. This is directly contrary to God's intention for us: He has ordained that we make Christ and our maturing in our relationship with Him to be our "life goal," and that our families be in God's order. Our relationships with our children and other family members should follow in priority our relationship with our spouses. Finally, we find the priority of our "ministry."

In each of these relationships, our first and primary responsibility is to allow *Christ in us* to minister unto others through us! Remember, *all ministry consists of our yielding to Christ within as love-motivated and Spirit-empowered servants,* that Christ in us might be glorified (i.e., made manifest to others through us). If we fail to first learn how to *serve* our closest family members, then we can forget about practicing it with other people!

A great deal of human suffering is caused by those in "ministry" who *reverse* these priorities. Many involved in Christian ministries experience severe (but usually well-covered-up) strains in their marriage relationship, and all of the problems that come when children are out of order. Furthermore, if the marriage relationship is of lower priority than one's "ministry," it does not give that "ministry" the necessary foundational support it needs, and the result is often at least burnout if not devastating satanic attack.

The time pressures of ministry often severely hinder ministers from spending the time they need with the Lord for the first priority, let alone all that follow. Many ministers find that they must keep their inner barriers against people well hidden to keep from being hurt by criticism. This is complicated by the fact that most of us never really know the *Sabbath rest* of the Lord.

2. Is Marriage a Prerequisite or a Hindrance to Ministry?

At first glance, the Bible seems to be somewhat contradictory on this question. Paul wrote extensively about the qualifications of elders or "overseers," and deacons in a local group of the Body of Christ. He also discussed marriage and whether or not a believer in ministry should marry (see 1 Tim. 3:1-5,12; 1 Cor. 7:1-3,6-9,20,24).

All who seek the total and perfect will of our Lord Christ Jesus for their lives should search their motives carefully. The time that marriage demands can strongly conflict with those of leadership ministry at times.

To help you seek understanding from Christ in you on this, we offer some following guidelines:

1. We can only function as a member of the Body of Christ utterly by faith—it is totally impossible except through Christ in us. This is also the only way to maintain our marriages according to scriptural principles.

2. Marriage is often used by our Lord to bring us to the point of living utterly by faith in Him, as we die to our self-seeking and self-protecting barriers. God uses our marriages as a testing ground to refine our faith in the indwelling Christ (see 1 Pet. 1:6-9), so that we will truly seek His lordship, even if our motives are only to alleviate the intense pains of our marriage conflicts and disappointments!

3. For many of the callings in the Body of Christ, marriage is indeed a valuable asset. Those are the callings that are geographically most settled and associated with one-to-one ministering; examples are those ministries involving counseling and local group leadership.

4. For many ministry callings, marriage is a liability. Those are the callings that are more geographically mobile, and most especially require living by faith without visible support; the evangelist, missionary, prophet, and apostle callings, for example.

5. As we just mentioned for all callings, the time that marriage demands often strongly conflict with those of leadership ministry. The burdens on the spouses and children of such ministers are intense. Only when all members of the family are united in one ministry as a team, will the ministry endure. Those who are in ministry based on the concept that only one member of the family has the ministry and the others are to support that one, are especially vulnerable to the attacks of satan in both the marriage and the ministry.

3. Women in the Body of Christ

Several years ago a wave of teachings flowed through the Body of Christ emphasizing that "we need to get our families in order." It emphasized the biblical admonition "husbands, love your wives; and wives, submit to your husbands" (see Eph. 5:24-25). This was a much-needed emphasis.

But that teaching also had an unduly degrading effect on many Christian women. Why? Because we failed to recognize several important principles:

1. God originally created Eve *fully equal to Adam* in her relationship to God and to Adam, though Adam and Eve were *different in nature* for a *specific purpose.*

2. God placed woman under the authority of her husband *solely as part of the Adamic curse.*

3. "In Christ," the Adamic curse—including woman's secondary relationship to her husband—*was and is nullified.*

4. Our families are brought into God's order not by a wife's blind obedience to her husband, but rather through the much more difficult step of *death to self*—in both husband and wife! The New Testament command for women to "submit" does not mean being under her husband in authority *per se,* but rather *being in oneness* with him *for God's purposes.*

4. Women in the New Testament Church

However one interprets the biblical admonition that "women keep silent in churches" (1 Cor. 14:34), *women were used extensively by our Lord Christ Jesus in leadership ministries* in the New Testament Church! This is documented throughout the Books of Acts, First Corinthians, Ephesians, Philippians, and First Timothy in particular.

There is neither male nor female in Christ *to the extent* that we minister by the Tree (readily available source) of

Life (Christ indwelling) in love-motivated and Spirit-empowered servanthood (see Gal. 3:28). Inversely, we are still under the Adamic curse *to the extent* that we minister by the Tree of Knowledge (self).

In Christ, men and women are *equal in value* though *different in nature.* Women in Christ have greater tendencies for social involvements than men (who in turn have greater tendencies for organizational accomplishments). For this reason, godly women tend to be more compassionate and concerned, and exhibit an even greater propensity for true love-motivated servanthood than men.

On the other hand, women outside of the indwelling Christ tend to manipulate others for personal acceptance. In extreme cases, women even fall under the influence of the satanic spirit of Jezebel. Again, the issue is the extent the indwelling Christ rules our hearts.

In every major text related to leadership ministries in the New Testament Church, *gender is not implied* in the original Greek. Only the all-inclusive generic neuter pronouns for "all"; "everyone"; "anyone"; and "each one" are used. The main cause for doctrinal confusion on this issue among serious Bible scholars is First Corinthians 11. There Paul addresses certain things that were wrong in the interpersonal relationships between members of the Corinthian church, including certain female believers who were using their feminine wiles to manipulate male believers for selfish ends. These women had to be regarded as still under the "law" for the time being. It is outside Christ's "headship" (a grossly inferior but all too common situation), that the law of "woman under husband" has relevance. It was for this reason Paul reminded that church of the position of women under the law in First Corinthians 11.

Since none of us are yet completely mature in Christ, we must still be dealt with and adjusted until we reach that maturity. Paul, under the inspiration of the Holy Spirit, gave this admonition as a matter of practical advice. But even there, his precise wording in the Greek allows women *who are truly living according to Christ indwelling* to be used by our Lord Christ Jesus in *leadership ministries.*

Birkey gives nine "theses" pertaining to the role of women in the New Testament Church. He notes the powerful ways our Lord Christ Jesus used women who were truly yielded to the indwelling Christ in leadership roles in the early churches:[3]

1. Women, alongside men, were full-membered participants in the Christian communities.

2. Women, side by side with men, were partners in leadership and ministry in the early churches.

3. Women, along with men, led in public prayer based on "likewise" in First Timothy 2:9: women "likewise" are to pray (the difference is men are to be without dissension and women are to be properly adorned).

4. Women, alongside men, prophesied in the church ("all" in First Corinthians 14:4,31 is genderless).

5. Women, with and in the presence of men, exhibited spiritual authority in the church body, i.e., by virtue of the presence of Christ in them.

6. Women in particular were encouraged to learn the Scriptures.

7. Women, even as men, had gifts for edifying the Body.

8. Wives as well as their husbands were partners in mutual submission, arising out of their mutual love.

9. Women's roles were not dichotomized or considered at variance with men's roles in Christ.

Birkey also lists numerous examples of women in leadership ministries in the early churches.

1. "Prominent women" (Acts 17:4,12).

2. Priscilla (Acts 18:18).

3. "He" in Romans 12:8 is *genderless* and *applies to women* as well as to men.

4. Phoebe, a *diakonos* or "deacon" (Rom. 16:1-2).

5. Junia (Rom. 16:7).

6. Mary, Tryphaena, Tryphosa, and Persis (Rom. 16:6,12).

7. Euodia and Syntyche (Phil. 4:2-3)[4]

All true ministries in the Body of Christ are forms of love-motivated servanthood that are possible only when empowered by the Spirit of Christ living within us. Therefore, regardless of what your calling is, it shares many things in common with all other callings. All callings in the Body of Christ have at least 14 common elements. They are the following:

1. They are forms of servanthood.

2. They are for the purpose of edifying others.

3. They are to be motivated out of love for others, not out of self-seeking of personal fulfillment.

4. They are empowered by the Spirit of Christ indwelling.

5. They are forms of leadership in the sense of influencing others.

6. They require personal subordination to all other members of the Body of Christ.

7. They require the Philippians 2:3 attitude toward all other members of the Body of Christ.

8. They have "walking in faith believing" as an important element.

9. They have intercession as an important element.

10. They have encouragement of others as an important element.

11. They have discernment of spirits as an important element.

12. They require intense mental discipline.

13. They require "reckoning one's self dead" to sin and to self-seeking.

14. They require honesty and effective unity with all other members of the Body of Christ.

End Notes: Chapter Twelve

1. Actually, God allows the conflicts and sufferings to occur in our lives as a refining fire in order to bring each of us, and our marriages, into a walk of faith in the indwelling Christ.

2. This is also true even on a national level. Virtually every war that has involved Western Europe and the United States had at its roots some national leader who honestly thought he was serving God by initiating the war!

3. Birkey, Del. *The House Church—A Model For Renewing The Church* (Scottdale, PA: Herald Press, 1988), pp. 91-102.

4. Ibid.

Epilogue:

It's Up to Us!

Whenever I momentarily lapse, get my attention off our Lord Christ Jesus, and view things purely with my natural mind, I am forced to be totally pessimistic about whether of not the full marriage relationship described in this volume is *actually* possible. This sixfold covenant of love-motivated servanthood, in *fullness,* is beyond my personal experience and/or observation to date. Even the most "Spirit-filled" Bible-believers whom I know well are far from experiencing such a marriage relationship.

We are still steeped in self-seeking. Our dysfunctionally rooted self-protecting goals, strategies, and behaviors are still much in place, maintaining distancing barriers within all interpersonal relationships, especially in our marriages. All of the ways husbands and wives act out self-seeking goals to protect themselves from the pain of inner emptiness are contrary to the God-ordained, harmonious, love-motivated servanthood paradigm of the marriage relationship.

It is *theoretically* possible for a marriage to get beyond this level and achieve this total intimacy, openness, and honesty with one another. But is it *actually* achievable?

Both partners must be or become free of all such self-seeking and self-protecting strategies, and free from fears of "discovery" leading to possible rejection. Most of us still have them deeply hidden. These powerfully dominate much of our thinking and actions in ways that we are mostly oblivious to.

From a worldly point of view, all of this seems hopeless. But if both spouses embrace the sanctifying workings of the indwelling Holy Spirit of Christ Jesus which we call "inner heart healing," then *such a marriage relationship is not only possible, but inevitable.* Much of that I *have* personally experienced! We cannot overemphasize the urgency of our embracing it!

Jeremiah 29:13 shouts to us today: "And you will seek Me and find Me, when you search for Me with all your heart." But it is only as we seek our Lord Christ Jesus *with our whole hearts—intensely, desperately—*that He is released to work in and through us. He commands us to *abide in Him,* and He has "filled" (saturated) our hearts with His Holy Spirit to empower us to abide in Him. His offer and responsibility is to abide in us! Then, and only then, are we truly messengers and agents of everything He has to our spouses and to others.

At this present time, each one of us is only as close to our Lord Christ Jesus, and to our spouse, that we are *choosing* to be. There is no *limit* as to how much closer we can come, both to Him and to our spouses, if we choose.

It's up to us!

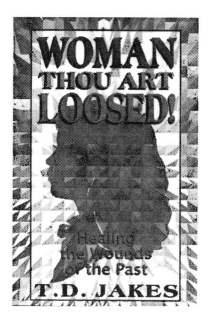

WOMAN, THOU ART LOOSED!

by T.D. Jakes.

This book offers healing to hurting single mothers, insecure women, and battered wives; and hope to abused girls and women in crisis! Hurting women around the nation—and those who minister to them—are devouring the compassionate truths in Bishop T.D. Jakes' *Woman, Thou Art Loosed!*

TPB-210p. ISBN 1-56043-100-8
Retail $9.99
A workbook is also available.
TPB-48p. ISBN 1-56043-810-X
Retail $6.99

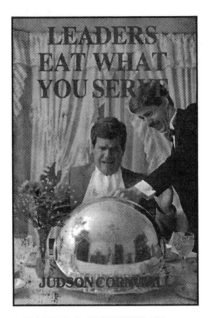

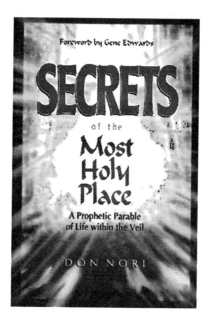

UNDERSTANDING YOUR POTENTIAL
by Myles Munroe.
This is a motivating, provocative look at the awesome potential trapped within you, waiting to be realized. This book will cause you to be uncomfortable with your present state of accomplishment and dissatisfied with resting on your past success.
TPB-168p. ISBN 1-56043-046-X Retail $8.99
Also available as a workbook.
TPB-48p. ISBN 1-56043-092-3
Retail $6.99

RELEASING YOUR POTENTIAL
by Myles Munroe.
Here is a complete, integrated, principles-centered approach to releasing the awesome potential trapped within you. If you are frustrated by your dreams, ideas, and visions, this book will show you a step-by-step pathway to releasing your potential and igniting the wheels of purpose and productivity.
TPB-182p. ISBN 1-56043-072-9 Retail $8.99
Also available as a workbook.
TPB-56p. ISBN 1-56043-093-1
Retail $6.99

IN PURSUIT OF PURPOSE
by Myles Munroe.
Best-selling author Myles Munroe reveals here the key to personal fulfillment: purpose. We must pursue purpose because our fulfillment in life depends upon our becoming what we were born to be and do. *In Pursuit of Purpose* will guide you on that path to finding purpose.
TPB-168p. ISBN 1-56043-103-2
Retail $8.99

SINGLE, MARRIED, SEPARATED & LIFE AFTER DIVORCE
by Myles Munroe.
Written by best-selling author Myles Munroe, this is one of the most important books you will ever read. It answers hard questions with compassion, biblical truth, and even a touch of humor. It, too, is rapidly becoming a best-seller.
TPB-140p. ISBN 1-56043-094-X Retail $7.99
Also available as a workbook.
TPB-48p. ISBN 1-56043-115-6 Retail $6.99